BU
151-

P9-AOK-340

THE
UNIVERS   F WINNIPEG
DISCARDED
PORTAGE &
WINNIPEG 2, MAN.   CANADA

THE NEW MERMAIDS

The Scottish History of James the Fourth

THE NEW MERMAIDS

General Editors

PHILIP BROCKBANK
Professor of English, York University

BRIAN MORRIS
Lecturer in English, York University

PR
2544
.S3
1967

The Scottish History of James the Fourth

ROBERT GREENE

Edited by J. A. LAVIN

ERNEST BENN LIMITED
LONDON

First published in this form 1967
by Ernest Benn Limited
Bouverie House · Fleet Street · London · EC4
© Ernest Benn Limited 1967
Distributed in Canada by
The General Publishing Company Limited · Toronto
Printed in Great Britain

CONTENTS

ACKNOWLEDGEMENTS

THE FOLLOWING EDITIONS have been consulted:

Alexander Dyce, ed., *The Dramatic Works of George Peele and Robert Greene* (London, 1861).

Alexander B. Grosart, ed., *The Life and Complete Works of Robert Greene*, The Huth Library (London, 1881–86), vol. XIII.

John Matthews Manly, ed., *Specimens of the Pre-Shaksperean Drama* (Boston, 1897), vol. II.

J. Churton Collins, ed., *The Plays and Poems of Robert Greene* (Oxford, 1905), 2 vols.

Thomas H. Dickinson, ed., *Robert Greene*, The Mermaid Series (London, 1909).

Ashley Thorndike, ed., *Minor Elizabethan Drama*, Everyman's Library (London, 1910), vol. II.

A. E. H. Swaen and W. W. Greg, eds., *The Scottish History of James the Fourth 1598*, Malone Society Reprints (London, 1921).

ABBREVIATIONS

THE FOLLOWING ABBREVIATIONS have been used in the notes:

Abbott, E. A. Abbott, *A Shakespearian Grammar* (London, 1870).

OED, *The Oxford English Dictionary*, 13 vols. (1933).

s.d. stage direction.

s.p. speech prefix.

Tilley, M. P. Tilley, *A Dictionary of the Proverbs in England in the Sixteenth and Seventeenth Centuries* (Michigan U.P., 1950).

INTRODUCTION

THE AUTHOR

IT IS GENERALLY accepted that an entry in the register of St. George, Tombland, recording the baptism of the second child of Robert Greene, a saddler, and Jane his wife, on 11 July 1558, refers to the dramatist Robert Greene. The signatures to *A Maiden's Dream*, 'R. Greene, Nordovicensis', and to the address to Lodge's *Euphues' Shadow*, 'Robert Greene Norfolciensis', support the conclusion that Greene was born in Norwich.

In *Modern Language Notes*, LXVI (1951), 546–549, Kenneth Mildenberger drew attention to an entry in the Cambridge University Register which records the matriculation of a Robert Greene, sizar, at Corpus Christi College in Easter term 1573. He thinks Greene 'undoubtedly attended the Free Grammar School' at Norwich, from which there were exhibitions to Corpus Christi, and that this entry refers to the poet. But we know that Greene matriculated as a sizar at St. John's in Michaelmas term 1575, and although a move from one college to another was not unusual, there was no need to matriculate twice.[1] Greene received his B.A. from St. John's on 22 January 1580, and his M.A. as a member of Clare in 1583. The dedication to the second part of *Mamillia* (entered in the Stationers' Register 6 September 1583) is signed 'from my Studie in Clare Hall the vij of Julie'. (The Stationers' Register entry of *Mamillia*, part one, on 3 October 1580, also makes it clear that Greene had begun to write euphuistic romances while still a student, perhaps while still an undergraduate.)

With the exception of the dates of publication of his works, the facts concerning the remainder of Greene's life are less certain. If we are to believe *The Repentance of Robert Greene*, he travelled to Italy and Spain, probably between the awarding of his B.A. in January 1580, and his entering Clare Hall. But the trip could have been made during any summer vacation between 1576 and 1582. Greene's pamphlets *Groatsworth of Wit*, *Never too Late*, *Mourning Garment*, and *The Repentance of Robert Greene*, contain autobiographical materials which help us to fill out the picture, though they must be used with caution.

---

[1] See Johnstone Parr, 'Robert Greene and his Classmates at Cambridge', *PMLA*, LXXVII (1962), p. 542.

From them it appears Greene married a gentleman's daughter in Norwich about 1585, but deserted her and went to London after she bore him a child. In London, and in need of money, he 'fell in amongst a company of players, who persuaded him to try his wit in writing of comedies, tragedies, or pastorals'. He wrote *Alphonsus, King of Aragon* about 1587, and in July 1588 was incorporated M.A. at Oxford. During this time he was also writing and selling euphuistic romances. *Friar Bacon and Friar Bungay* was completed about 1589, and *A Looking-Glass for London and England* with Thomas Lodge the following year. Greene may also have written or assisted with *George-a-Greene* in 1590. The first and second parts of *Conny-catching* were published in 1591, and Greene's last two plays *Orlando Furioso* and *James IV* were probably written the same year. In 1592 *A Quip for an Upstart Courtier* was published, in which Greene attacked the Harveys, replying to a pamphlet by Richard Harvey entitled *The Lamb of God*, which had called writers 'piperly make-plays and make-bates'. Greene died, poverty-stricken, aged thirty-four, in London on 2 or 3 September 1592, before the Harveys' answer appeared, Gabriel Harvey's *Four Letters* (1592). The latter work gives an account of the death of Greene, 'in a shoemakers house near Dow-gate . . . of a surfett of pickle herringe and rennish wine'. According to Harvey, Greene employed a ruffian named Cutting Ball as a bodyguard, and kept Ball's sister as his mistress, by whom he had an illegitimate son, Fortunatus. Harvey alleges that Greene owed the shoemaker Isam ten pounds, that he wrote a letter on his death-bed asking his wife Doll to pay the debt, and that his hose, doublet, and sword were sold for three shillings to help defray the cost of burial in the New Churchyard near Bedlam.

In the year he died Greene's *Groatsworth of Wit* was published. In a prefatory letter addressed 'To those Gentlemen his Quondam acquaintance, that spend their wits in making plays', occurs Greene's famous reference to Shakespeare:

> Yes trust them not: for there is an vpstart Crow, beautified with our feathers, that with his *Tygers hart wrapt in a Players hyde*, supposes he is as well able to bombast out a blanke verse as the best of you: and being an absolute Iohannes fac totum, is in his owne conceit the onely Shake-scene in a countrey. O that I might intreat your rare wits to be imploied in more profitable courses.

Scholars agree that these lines refer to Shakespeare; Greene's parody of a line from *3 Henry VI*, 'O tiger's heart wrapp'd in a woman's hide' (I. iv, 137), supports this conclusion, but the precise meaning of the passage is still being debated. Peter Alexander, *Shakespeare's Henry VI and Richard III* (Cambridge, 1929), p. 44, suggested that Greene is merely warning his fellow playwrights against the ungrateful actors. This view, repeated by Alexander in *Shakespeare's Life and Art* (London, 1939), p. 52, was until recently accepted by most scholars (see E. K. Chambers, *William Shakespeare* (Oxford, 1930, I. 217; W. W. Greg, *The Editorial Problem in Shakespeare*, Oxford, 1942, p. 51; T. W. Baldwin, *On the Literary Genetics of Shakspere's Plays 1592–1594*, Urbana, 1959, 47–49). However, J. Dover Wilson, 'Malone and the Upstart Crow' in *Shakespeare Survey*, IV (1951), 56–68, and Sidney Thomas, 'The Meaning of Greene's Attack on Shakespeare', *Modern Language Notes*, LXVI (1951), 483–484, argue that Greene's phraseology might well have been interpreted by Elizabethans as an accusation of plagiarism. The debate continues; P. G. Nilsson, 'The Upstart Crow and Henry VI', *Moderna Sprak*, LVIII (1964), 293–303, for instance, argues that Greene's resentment of Shakespeare was caused, not by Shakespeare's revision of a play by Greene or Nashe, but by a collaboration in which Shakespeare was too aggressive.

Greene was a prolific writer, better known in his own day for his fiction than for his plays. Before his death thirty-six of his pamphlets and euphuistic romances were printed, and some of them were frequently reprinted, *Pandosto* (the source of *The Winter's Tale*) being one of the most popular. Four plays are certainly by him; he definitely assisted with one other, and may well have helped with more.

The only complete edition of Greene's work (unfortunately inaccurate) is that edited by A. B. Grosart, *The Life and Complete Works of Robert Greene* (Huth Library, 1881–86), reissued by Russell and Russell Inc., New York (1964). The standard (but untrustworthy) edition of the plays and poems is that by J. Churton Collins in 2 vols. (Oxford, 1905). The most recent biography, and the fullest consideration of Greene's prose works, is R. Pruvost's *Robert Greene et ses Romans* (Paris, 1938). S. A. Tannenbaum compiled a bibliography, *Elizabethan Bibliographies No. 8: Robert Greene* (New York, 1939), and a supplement to it (1945).

THE PLAY

The exact date of composition of *James IV* is not known, but it is regarded as Greene's most mature play; the exposition is skilful, there is less literary allusion than in his other plays, rhyme is used functionally, and the influence of Marlowe has receded (see Una Ellis-Fermor, 'Marlowe and Greene: A Note on their Relations as Dramatic Artists', *Studies in Honor of T. W. Baldwin*, ed. D. C. Allen, Urbana, 1958, 136–149). It is therefore usually assigned to 1591, though on the slim evidence of the title-page motto, T. W.

Baldwin, following F. G. Fleay's arguments in *A Biographical Chronicle of the English Drama 1559–1642* (London, 1891), I, 265, dates the play 'not later than 1590, hardly later than the summer' (*Literary Genetics*, p. 66). Despite the title-page claim, there is no record of the play having been performed in the sixteenth century, and it is not mentioned by Henslowe, who owned Greene's other plays.

On 14 May 1594 Thomas Creede entered *The Famous Victories of Henry V* in the Stationers' Register, and *James IV* also:

> Entred vnto him by the like warrant a booke intituled the Scottishe story of Iames the ffourthe slayne at Fflodden intermixed with a plesant Comedie presented by Oboron kinge of ffayres.   vj^d
> (*Arber*, II, 648)

No edition of *James IV* is known before that of 1598, and it would be natural to assume that the original edition had not survived, but for the fact that 1598 is also the date of the earliest known edition of *The Famous Victories*. In the circumstances it appears that publication of the two plays was for some reason delayed. The 1598 edition of *James IV* is a quarto printed by Creede in roman type, with stage-directions in italic. Creede also printed *A Looking-Glass for London and England* (1594), and *Alphonsus, King of Aragon* (1599). There are four known exemplars of *James IV*, those in the British Museum, the Folger Shakespeare Library, the Henry E. Huntington Library, and the Victoria and Albert Museum, which have been collated for the present edition. The quarto was carelessly printed; previous editors have commented at length on the badness of the text (for a list of errors, see the Malone Society Reprint, ed. A. E. H. Swaen and W. W. Greg, 1921).

Despite the assertions of Collins, 'The text is in a very bad state, and has evidently been printed, without any attempt at editing, from a stage copy' (it is not clear whether he meant a prompt-book); and Dickinson, 'The text of the quarto of 1598 is in very poor state, and shows indications that the play was either published from a stage copy or that type was set by dictation', the play bears all the marks of having been printed from Greene's foul papers.

Matters that would have been cleared up in a prompt-book are left confused in *James IV*: Arius is used as the name both of the King of England and the King of Scotland; ghost characters Lords Percy and Samles are listed in the initial s.d. of V. iii, though Douglas, who has a speaking part in that scene, is not; and the designation of characters is irregular, both in s.d.'s and s.p.'s, Ateukin sometimes being called Gnato, and Nano sometimes Dwarf. Stage directions are descriptive of appearance: 'Bohan a Scot, attired like a Ridstall man'; of status: 'Dorothea his Queen'; of grouping: 'Ateukin with them aloof'; of location: 'in their porch'; of attitude: 'They all are in a muse'; and disguise is noted: 'Dorothea in man's apparel'; but more significant are the permissive and indefinite directions: 'a tomb, placed conveniently on the stage'; 'a jig devised for the nonce'; 'a round of fairies, or some pretty dance'; 'with a companion, boy or wench'; 'enter certain huntsmen, if you please, singing'; 'enter a round, or some dance at pleasure'; 'enter from the widow's house a service, musical songs of marriages, or a masque, or what pretty triumph you list'; all these are indicative of an authorial MS.

Kenneth Muir has pointed to other 'weaknesses' which may or may not indicate that the play was never revised for production. According to Muir, 'Robert Greene as Dramatist', *Essays on Shakespeare and Elizabethan Drama in Honor of Hardin Craig*, ed. Richard Hosley (Columbia, 1962), p. 50:

> It is absurd for Bohan's sons to appear as characters in the play he is presenting before Oberon, especially as the events are supposed to have taken place in an earlier age; it is artistically confusing when Slipper is rescued from the gallows by the intervention of Oberon; and Greene does not explain how Nano, who takes service with Ateukin in the first act, should be in Dorothea's service in the second.

The last statement is incorrect, see I. ii, 119: 'Then will I deck thee princely, instruct thee courtly, and present thee to the queen as my gift.' The first two points may be answered by asserting that it is useless to criticize Greene for his unrealistic handling of what is a completely unrealistic device—the 'sit and see' framework of the play. Muir's further stricture, 'the scenes in which Lady Anderson falls in love with the disguised Dorothea are bungled', is answered by the text of this edition.

Despite the title-page and Induction references to James IV, the play is entirely unhistorical, being derived from the first novel of the third day of Giraldi Cinthio's *Hecatomithi*;[1] Greene may also have known Cinthio's dramatization of the story, *Arrenopia*. Churton Collins in his edition of Greene's *Plays and Poems* gives 'a brief analysis of the novel with extracts' (II, 80–83). Greene makes his central character King of Scotland, rather than of Ireland, as he is in the novel. The war in the play is thus fought between England and Scotland, instead of between Ireland and Scotland, as in Cinthio.

---

[1] See P. A. Daniel's announcement of this discovery (*Athenaeum*, 8 October 1881, p. 465); W. Creizenach (*Anglia*, VIII (1885), p. 419), seems to have reached the same conclusion independently.

This permits Greene to make comments on the desirability of amicable relations, if not union, between England and Scotland. He also condenses the lengthy development of the king's infatuation, and melodramatically makes him fall in love with Ida (the sole name retained from the novel) at the very moment of his marriage, at which point the play proper opens. Greene minimises the king's guilt by having the murder of his wife suggested to him, instead of the king planning it himself, as in the novel. Nor does the king accuse her of adultery as in Cinthio. The Bohan-Oberon framework is Greene's invention, as are the dumb-shows.

Greene had used a framework with inset stories in several of his romances, giving them the form of a *débat*, and in the play also the Bohan-Oberon framework is used to introduce what is essentially a dramatized exemplum; Bohan's 'jig' (the play itself) is intended to show 'whay I hate the world, by demonstration'. The choruses between the acts point the moral further:

Then mark my stay, and the strange doubts,
That follow flatterers, lust and lawless will,
And then say I have reason to forsake
The world, and all that are within the same. (I. Chorus 10–13)

                     . . . his flatterers,
Sweetening his thoughts of luckless lust,
With vile persuasions and alluring words,
Makes him make way by murther to his will.
Judge fairy king, hast heard a greater ill? (II. Chorus 4–8)

For it would make a marble melt and weep
To see these treasons 'gainst the innocent (III. Chorus 3–4)

Mark thou my jig, in mirkest terms that tells
The loath of sins, and where corruption dwells. (V. Chorus 5–6)

But although Bohan is represented as the author as well as presenter of the play:

OBERON
Believe me bonny Scot, these strange events
Are passing pleasing, may they end as well.
BOHAN
Else say that Bohan hath a barren skull,
If better motions yet than any past
Do not more glee to make the fairy greet, (IV. Chorus 1–5)

and although Oberon promises (IV. Chorus 13–14) to exercise those magical powers which he has demonstrated in the Induction, and does in fact intervene in the action to save Slipper from hanging (V. vi, 57), magic is not used to guide the narrative, as in *Friar Bacon*, nor even as in *Orlando Furioso*, where Melissa's magic ends

Orlando's furiosity. Apart from choric comments, the framework is used by Greene as an excuse for the introduction of inter-act jigs, hornpipes, and rounds, which are extraneous to the play. Within the play itself use is also made of music, song, dance, and spectacle which is essentially non-functional (e.g. the two hunting scenes in Act IV), though in the second hunting scene Greene's interest in emblems (see the emblematic verses in his *Alcida*) leads him to make use of a well-known emblem, 'Silver hart with arrow wounded', on which he moralises in conventional fashion.

It is a critical cliché that Greene showed Shakespeare what could be done with romantic comedy: 'In Oberon we have the germ of a Prospero, in Bohan the germ of a Jaques' (Collins, II, 83); 'His induction serves as a model for Shakespeare's *Taming of the Shrew*; and one of its characters, Oberon, is a rough draft for the fairy of that name in *A Midsummer Night's Dream*, as Bohan is a prototype of Jaques in *As You Like It*' (Dickinson, p. lxi). But it can as easily be argued that *James IV* is a transitional Morality as that it is an early Romantic Comedy. The King of Scots goes through the spiritual odyssey of the morality from innocence to degeneracy and eventual repentance and regeneration. As in the morality his good and bad acquaintances are either tempters or supporters in the journey towards salvation. His chief tempter, Ateukin, has not moved very far along the road of dramatic development from the allegorical figure of the Vice himself, and indeed is occasionally referred to by the label-name Gnato (a sycophant in Terence's *Eunuchus*). Not many years earlier, as the evil protagonist of the Psychomachia plot, he would have been called Flattery, Lust, or Politic Persuasion.

In this play, however, he is first represented as an astrologer, though after his initial appearance we hear no more of astrology, and he is given the conventional attributes of the Machiavel and vicious flatterer. (Waldo F. McNeir, 'Ateukin in Greene's *James IV*', *Modern Language Notes*, LXII, 1947, 376–381, claims that the character is based on John Damian, alchemist to the historical James IV.) Ateukin has made annotations on Machiavelli (III. ii, 51; like Flowerdale in *The London Prodigal*), and with Machiavellian shrewdness argues from absolutism to the necessity of murder:

> You are the king, the state depends on you:
> Your will is law, say that the case were mine,
> Were she my sister whom your highness loves,
> She should consent, for that our lives, our goods,
> Depend on you . . .
> But if the lamb should let the lion's way,
> By my advice the lamb should lose her life.   (I. i, 248–256)

He later twists a proverbial saying from Aristotle to support the argument:

> Why prince, it is no murther in a king
> To end another's life to save his own.   (IV. v, 35–36)

and uses the conventional analogy between state and body to justify his murderous 'policy' (IV. v, 45–48).

After his first appearance, on which, after eavesdropping, he pretends to read the king's thoughts, Ateukin is presented by Greene as the epitome of the flatterer. But his very first words are self-conscious flattery (I. i, 183–184), though he claims to be neither parasite (line 226), nor flatterer (270 ff.), a pose he continues to employ. His establishment in the king's favour, and the public danger of such flatterers, is commented on by other characters (II. ii, 48; III. ii, 26–27: 'The world is at a wise pass, when nobility is afraid of a flatterer.'), while murder, corruption, and double-dealing are shown to be the consequences (III. iii, 18; 52–57). The social order is overturned, as Sir Bartram remarks (III. iii, 50), and as is demonstrated by Andrew and Jaques resisting the king's purveyor (III. ii, 1–47). Andrew himself comments on the new conditions at Court, and determines to do some double-dealing on his own account (IV. v, 80–97), 'As I am sure long flattery cannot hold.'

When Ateukin's plots fail, he soliloquises on the evils of flattery (V. ii, 9–21), briefly considers the possibility of murdering Eustace, is deserted by Jaques, reviews his own sycophantic career, shows remorse, and concludes by pointing the moral:

> Thus God doth work with those, that purchase fame
> By flattery, and make their prince their gain.   (V. ii, 39–40)

In the reconciliation scene with which the play ends, the viciousness of the flatterer is further emphasised, and it is he, rather than the king, who is censured:

> As for Ateukin, and his lewd compeers,
> That soothed you in your sins and youthly pomp,
> Exile, torment, and punish such as they,
> For greater vipers never may be found
> Within a state, than such aspiring heads,
> That reck not how they climb, so that they climb.
>   (V. vi, 200–205)

The king then asks pardon of Sir Cuthbert, the queen, and the nobles, agrees to 'embrace and reconcile' his good counsellors, and gives orders for Ateukin's capture and execution.

The close connection of *James IV* with the morality tradition may have been understressed by the critics because it is not a homiletic

tragedy, such as *Dr. Faustus*, but is in fact a homiletic comedy. It
thus belongs to an earlier tradition than the intermediate moralities
of the 1560's and 1570's, with their pattern of spiritual defeat and
damnation, and Greene even retains the early dramatic device of the
hero's dismissal of his guides to spiritual recovery (II. ii), but
reminds us of the norms of moral behaviour through the choric comments of Bohan and Oberon.

James IV is nevertheless linked to those intermediate moralities
which were hybrid chronicles and romances. In the framework
Greene brings together the fairy king from *Huon of Bordeaux* and a
very human Timonist Scot, while in the play itself Greene splits
the Capitano of his Italian source into two barely-disguised allegorical figures from the Psychomachia, Ateukin the Vice and Slipper his
vice lieutenant. At the same time Greene attempts to place these
figures of romance and allegory in a historical context (the title-page
references to James IV may not be Greene's; those in the Induction
must be), but without real effort.

A relic of the vice lieutenant's quarrels for supremacy with the
Vice may be seen in the attitude towards, and insulting of, Ateukin
by Slipper (II. i), and by Andrew (III. ii); Andrew's stealing of
Slipper's purse (IV. iii) belongs to the same tradition. But the comic
relief such characters and episodes provide is also functional; the
comedians point the moral of the main plot not only by reflecting
the degeneracy of society which the behaviour of the protagonist has
caused (e.g. the Purveyor scene, III. ii), but also overtly by directly
addressing the audience:

> Oh what a trim world is this! My master lives by cozening the king,
> I by flattering him: Slipper my fellow by stealing, and I by lying: is
> not this a wily accord, gentlemen?   (IV. iii, 20–23)

Though Greene does not develop in *James IV* a coherent subplot
of the kind found in later Elizabethan plays, this parallel relationship
of comedians to hero is brought out clearly; as Andrew says to
Ateukin:

> Is it flattery in me sir to speak you fair? What is it then in you to
> dally with the king?   (III. ii, 69–70)

It should also be noted that as in *Much Ado About Nothing*, the
main plot is directly affected by the actions of characters in the
subplot; Slipper's theft of the East Spring documents puts into Sir
Bartram's hands the warrant for Dorothea's death, and allows Greene
to introduce the disguise motif and the duelling scene (similar in
essence to the Viola-Aguecheek duel in *Twelfth Night*). A dramatic
possibility provided by the disguised heroine, later carried further

by Shakespeare, is touched on lightly by Greene in the scenes between the infatuated Lady Anderson and Dorothea (cf. Viola and Olivia). The main plot is further affected by Andrew's letter to the King of England, which apparently precipitates the war, and brings the eventual happy conclusion.

The moral debate of the Merchant, the Lawyer, and the Divine in V. iv fits neatly into a view of *James IV* as a late morality. They appear without explanation and are dismissed from the play in the same fashion once their homiletic function is complete. Such handling of genuinely allegorical personifications is typical of the moral drama, and though in *James IV* these figures are merely generalised types generically named, rather like Commons' Cry and Commons' Complaint in *Cambises*, their specific purpose as commentators on the progress of the exemplum is clear. It is this obsolescent dramatic method which has caused the scene to be suspected as 'an interpolation from some other drama' (Collins, II, 79); T. M. Parrott says the scene 'has no bearing on the action and is so unlike Greene's style as to suggest that it may have been inserted by some moralising reviser of the script' (*Shakespearean Comedy*, 1949, p. 85); while Muir remarks that the scene 'which was presumably intended to illustrate the evil results of James IV's misgovernment, is never once brought into focus' ('Robert Greene as Dramatist', p. 50). We should remember that in *Friar Bacon* also, Greene makes use of a traditional piece of stage business derived from the moralities, when Bungay and Miles are carried off on the devil's back (vi, 170; xvi, 63).

Despite the praise that has been heaped upon them,[2] the women

---

[2] See J. A. Symonds, *Shakspere's Predecessors in the English Drama* (new ed., 1900), p. 448: 'Fawnia in *Pandosto*, Margaret in *Friar Bacon*, Sephestia in *Menaphon*, Ida and Dorothea in *James the Fourth*, Philomela and the Shepherd's Wife in the *Mourning Garment*, belong to one sisterhood, in whom the innocence of country life, unselfish love, and maternity are sketched with delicate and feeling touches'; J. Churton Collins, *The Plays and Poems of Robert Greene* (Oxford, 1905), II, 84: 'Dorothea would do honour to Shakespeare: she is the soul of the drama, and as her presence pervades it she redeems all the faults of the play'; Thomas H. Dickinson, *Robert Greene* (London, 1909), p. lxiii: 'And in the depiction of women Greene lavishes the finest forces of his genius . . . Nothing in Marlowe . . . can equal the sweet and simple womanliness of Greene's gallery'; Ashley Thorndike, *Minor Elizabethan Drama* (London, 1910), II, xi: 'To his heroines, Ida and Dorothea, however, he gave his best efforts, and they remind us again and again of Shakespeare's women . . . Greene's characterisation is altogether sympathetic and winning'; C. F. Tucker Brooke, *The Tudor Drama* (Cambridge, Mass., 1911), p. 266: 'It is generally agreed that the chief merit of Greene's romantic plays . . . lies in the character of his

characters of the play are little more than personifications of feminine
virtue, hardly developed as personalities in their own right. As with
the casual introduction and disposition of the Lawyer, the Merchant,
and the Divine, so with the handling of Ida and Dorothea. Neither is
psychologically motivated, their function in the play being purely
exemplary. Both derive from the traditional figure of medieval and
Renaissance romance, Patient Griselda, the archetype of extreme
and almost miraculous steadfastness. In *Friar Bacon* Greene had
already employed this figure (in the character of Margaret of
Fressingfield) in a similar fashion, her successful withstanding of the
test of her constancy leading to the establishment of that order and
happiness in the state with which all Greene's plays end (either
through marriage, or the reunion or reconciliation of lovers).

In Ida, unmarried chastity is tested by the king's threats and
bribes ('He shall erect your state and wed you well.' II. i, 142),
prefaced by a discussion between mother and daughter which not
only makes clear Ida's moral position, but which hammers home
moral generalities:

> But those that prank on top of fortune's ball,
> Still fear a change: and fearing catch a fall. (II. i, 11–12)

which are further given a Christian cast:

> God with a beck can change each worldly thing,
> The poor to rich, the beggar to the king. (II. i, 27–28)

Her successful resistance to the king's importunities proves Ida
worthy of the noble love of Eustace.

The testing of Dorothea's constancy follows the basic Griselda
story more closely. Not only does she refuse to see the faults in her

---

heroines'; J. M. Robertson, *Elizabethan Literature* (London, 1914), p. 105;
'Dorothea . . . forecasts the noblest types of womanhood in Shakespeare';
J. C. Jordan, *Robert Greene* (New York, 1915), p. 197: 'His imagination when
dealing with women characters was able to bring forth creatures for whom
his reader can feel genuine interest and sympathy'; Allardyce Nicoll,
British Drama (London, 1925), p. 90: '[Dorothea is] the best-drawn woman
figure in sixteenth-century drama outside Shakespeare's comedies'; T. M.
Parrott and R. H. Ball, *A Short View of Elizabethan Drama* (New York,
1943), p. 73: 'And he deserves more than a little credit for his characterisation
of the two ladies who figure in the play, the chaste and gentle Ida and the
devoted Dorothea . . . More fully realised, lifelike, and credible than the
shadowy women of Lyly's plays . . .'; T. M. Parrott, *Shakespearean Comedy*
(New York, 1949), p. 86: 'His Ida is a true and charming portrait of the
Elizabethan girl . . . The character of the Queen, however, is Greene's
supreme achievement.'

husband which are so obvious to the nobles (II. ii, 47–56), but she actually interprets the king's attentions to Ida in terms of the Griselda story:

Ah Douglas thou misconstrest his intent,
He doth but tempt his wife, he tries my love.   (II. ii, 84–85)

She refuses to believe that an order has been given for her death, because

. . . love the faithful link of loyal hearts,
That hath possession of my constant mind,
Exiles all dread, subdueth vain suspect.   (III. iii, 4–6)

and when shown the warrant, suggests that it may be a forgery. Convinced by the hand and seal, she is immediately ready to forgive the king:

But oh mine eyes, were you as bent to hide,
As my poor heart is forward to forgive,
Ah cruel king, my love would thee acquit.   (III. iii, 71–73)

and remonstrates with Ross when he promises to avenge her:

What then can conquer him that kills not me?   (III. iii, 87)

She faints with grief on hearing that the nobles have deserted her husband (V. i, 65), and when Lady Anderson advises her to return to her father, replies with a speech that is psychologically unrealistic, but which has an important place in the development of the moral:

Ah lady, so would worldly counsel work,
But constancy, obedience, and my love,
In that my husband is my lord and chief,
These call me to compassion of his estate,
Dissuade me not, for virtue will not change.   (V. v, 67–71)

Lady Anderson's reply is equally significant:

What wondrous constancy is this I hear?
If English dames their husbands love so dear,
I fear me in the world they have no peer.   (V. v, 72–74)

In the final scene of the play Dorothea's summary of the near-tragic consequences of her husband's infatuation, spoken as she stands between opposing armies, is hardly realistic:

Shame me not prince, companion in thy bed,
Youth hath misled: tut, but a little fault,
'Tis kingly to amend what is amiss.   (V. vi, 159–161)

Dorothea, then, is an emblem rather than a realistically motivated character.

Despite the misanthropy of Bohan, and Oberon's approval of that attitude in the framework, and despite their contention that the plot of the play supports such a view of the world, the play itself points a quite different moral. Human love is seen as the power which can overcome fortune and restore the natural order in both the individual and the realm. The charity of Sir Cuthbert Anderson is another variety of Dorothea's charity towards her husband, and together they succeed in reclaiming the young prodigal, whose repentance permits his forgiveness. Notably, the *ubi sunt* and *memento mori* themes of the three dumb-shows presented by Oberon, do not correspond to the outcome of the play proper; the lesson they teach about worldly pomp is only relevant in a general way to a tragi-comedy concerning flattery and lust, in which the king survives to live happily, unlike the monarchs of the dumb-shows. The dumb-shows illustrate human folly; in the play itself folly is redeemed.

NOTE ON THE TEXT

THIS EDITION IS based on the quarto text of *James IV*, printed by Thomas Creede in 1598. Photostats of the Folger copy were used as the control text, collated with microfilms of the three other known exemplars, those in the British Museum (c. 34. g. 20), the Victoria and Albert Museum (4247. 18. k. 17), and the Huntington Library (61133). Thirty-one minor press variants were identified, in addition to many errors in the facsimile leaf A4 of the BM copy, and several errors in the facsimile corner of leaf H in the VA copy.

The present edition is the first to benefit from a collation of all four surviving copies of the quarto, and differs from its predecessors in three other ways, apart from minor corrections to the text. It places the alternative dumb-shows after the play proper, instead of after the first act; it places what is clearly the concluding chorus of the play in its proper position, instead of after the first act; and it changes the position of a single speech by Dorothea within V. v to clear up the confusion of that scene.

FURTHER READING

Baldwin, T. W. *On the Literary Genetics of Shakspere's Plays 1592–1594* (Urbana, 1959).

Bevington, David M. *From Mankind to Marlowe* (Cambridge, Mass., 1962).

Bradbrook, M. C. *The Growth and Structure of Elizabethan Comedy* (London, 1955).

Ellis-Fermor, Una. 'Marlowe and Greene: A Note on Their Relations as Dramatic Artists', in *Studies in Honor of T. W. Baldwin*, ed. D. C. Allen (Urbana, 1958).

Jordan, J. C. *Robert Greene* (New York, 1915).

Muir, Kenneth. 'Robert Greene as Dramatist', in *Essays on Shakespeare and Elizabethan Drama in Honor of Hardin Craig*, ed. Richard Hosley (Columbia, 1962).

Pettet, E. C. 'The Comedies of Greene', in his *Shakespeare and the Romance Tradition* (London, 1949).

Pruvost, René. *Robert Greene et ses Romans* (Paris, 1938).

Rossiter, A. P. *English Drama from Early Times to the Elizabethans* (London, 1950).

Sanders, Norman. 'The Comedy of Greene and Shakespeare', in *Early Shakespeare*, Stratford-upon-Avon Studies 3, ed. John Russell Brown and Bernard Harris (London, 1961).

THE
SCOTTISH
Historie of Iames the

fourth, slaine at *Flodden*.

Entermixed with a pleasant Comedie, presented by
Oboram King of *Fayeries:*

*As it hath bene sundrie times publikely
plaide.*

Written by *Robert Greene*, Maister of Arts.

Omne tulit punctum.

LONDON
Printed by Thomas Creede. 1598.

Omne tulit punctum. From Horace, *De Arte Poeticae*, 343–344:
>Omne tulit punctum, qui miscuit utile dulci
>Lectorem delectando, pariterque monendo

(He gains universal applause who mingles the useful with the agreeable, at once delighting and instructing the reader; i.e. the writer who can combine instruction with amusement is worthy of praise.) *Omne . . . dulci* appeared on the title-pages of *Arbasto* (1584), *Penelopes Web* (1587), *Pandosto* (1588), *Perimedes* (1588), in which Greene calls it his 'old poesie' (sig. A3), and *Ciceronis Amor* (1589), and at the end of *Friar Bacon* (1594). *Omne . . . punctum* was used for *Menaphon* (1589), *Never Too Late* (1590), *James IV* (1598), and *Orpharion* (1599). The motto had previously appeared on the title-page of Pettie's *Petite Pallace*, from which Greene borrowed material for his prose. It came to be regarded as Greene's motto, cf. *The Return from Parnassus* I (1598?), lines 209–212: 'But if thou haste ere an Omne tulit punctū, ere a *Magister artiū vtriusque Academiae*, ere an *Opus* and *Vsus*, ere a needie Pamphlet, drincke of a sentence to vs, to the health of mirth and the confusion of Melancholye.' Greene's use of it is referred to by *Nashe*, I. 10. 25, when attacking certain authors in his *Anatomie of Absurditie* (1589): 'Are they not ashamed in their prefixed posies, to adorne a pretence of profit mixt with pleasure.' Harvey, in *Foure Letters* (1592), *Wks*, I, 189, refers to it as 'his professed Poesie'.

[Characters of the Play

OBERON, King of Fairies
BOHAN, a malcontent Scot
SLIPPER, a Clown, servant to ATEUKIN ⎱ sons to BOHAN
NANO, a Dwarf, servant to DOROTHEA ⎰
KING OF SCOTS
ATEUKIN
ANDREW SNOORD, servant to ATEUKIN
SIR BARTRAM ⎫
BISHOP OF ST. ANDREWS ⎪
DOUGLAS ⎬ Scottish Lords
MORTON ⎪
ROSS ⎪
SIR CUTHBERT ANDERSON ⎭
PURVEYOR to the KING OF SCOTS
A Scottish SCOUT
JAQUES, a Frenchman
KING OF ENGLAND
EUSTACE ⎫
PERCY ⎬ English Lords
SAMLES ⎭
English HERALD
A TAILOR, a SHOEMAKER, a CUTLER
A LAWYER, a MERCHANT, a DIVINE
DOROTHEA, Queen of Scots
COUNTESS OF ARRAN
IDA, her daughter
LADY ANDERSON
Antics, Lords, Ladies, Fairies, Servants, Huntsmen,
Masquers, Soldiers.]

[Induction]

THE SCOTTISH
History of James the
fourth, slain at *Flodden*

Music playing within. Enter after OBERON, *King of Fairies, an antic, who dance about a tomb, placed conveniently on the stage, out of the which, suddenly starts up as they dance,* BOHAN *a Scot, attired like a Redesdale man, from whom the antic flies.*
OBERON *manet*

---

s.d. *after* ed. (Q Aster)
an antic a group of grotesquely costumed dancers
Redesdale man ed. (Q *Ridstall man*) wild man

---

s.d. *a tomb . . . stage.* Cf. Glynne Wickham, *Early English Stages 1300 to 1660*, II. i, p. 318: 'It is possible that the Antics carried this tomb with them from the tiring-house, put it down on the stage and danced round it, but the wording actually used suggests that the tomb had been placed in a convenient position by the stage management before the action began . . . As this place of concealment is later referred to by Bohun [*sic*] as "our arbour", it is permissible to suppose that this tomb, like Farrington's in the Lord Mayor's Show of 1616, was constructed in the style of an arbour and that the "gallery" was the balustraded, upper-storey of the tomb.' The latter part of this statement is incorrect; see footnote to I. Chorus, 14. It is 'the gallery' to which Bohan later refers as 'our harbour' and 'our cell', *not* the tomb. Tombs were used in several plays, and Henslowe bought two in 1598 (W. W. Greg, *Henslowe Papers*, p. 116). Wickham thinks Bohan's tomb was used as Cyrus' monument in the second dumb-show.
s.d. *a Redesdale man.* The emendation was suggested by W. L. Renwick, *MLR* xxix (1934), p. 434, later supported by H. G. Wright, *MLR* xxx (1935), p. 437, and J. C. Maxwell, *MLR* xliv (1949), p. 88, who quotes from Thomas Wilson's *Arte of Rhetorique* (p. 93 of G. H. Mair's edition): 'His soyle also (where he was borne) giueth him to bee an euill man: considering he was bredde and brought vp among a denne of Theeues, among the men of Tinsdale & Riddesdale, where pillage is good purchase, and murthering is coumpted manhood.' Thus *a Redesdale man* would have a wild, ferocious appearance.

5

BOHAN

Ay say, what's thou?

OBERON

Thy friend Bohan.

BOHAN

What wot I, or reck I that, whay guid man, I reck no friend,
nor ay reck no foe, all's ene to me, git thee ganging, and
trouble not may whayet, or ay's gar thee reckon me nene of   5
thay friend, by the mary mass sall I.

OBERON

Why angry Scot, I visit thee for love: then what moves thee
to wrath?

BOHAN

The de'il a whit reck I thy love, for I know too well, that
true love took her flight twenty winter sence to heaven,   10
whither till ay can, weel I wot, ay sall ne'er find love: an
thou lovest me, leave me to myself. But what were those
puppets that hopped and skipped about me year whayle?

OBERON

My subjects.

BOHAN

Thay subjects, whay, art thou a king?   15

OBERON

I am.

 1 *Ay* I
 3 *wot* know
   reck care for
 4 *ene* one
   ganging going
 5 *whayet* quiet
   ay's gar I'll make
   nene none
 6 *mary mass* a mass in honour of the Virgin Mary (a common
   sixteenth-century oath)
11 *love* BM HN VA *loves* Folger
13 *puppets* performers (this instance is the earliest example cited by
   OED)   *year whayle* erewhile

---

 1 *Ay.* Greene or the compositor was inconsistent in the use of *I* or the
   Scotticism *Ay* in Bohan's lines. This ed. follows Q. See J. O. Bartley,
   Teague, Shenkin and Sawney (Cork, 1954), p. 85: 'Bohan's dialect is
   well marked, though not consistent, in the induction; in the interlude
   between first and second acts his speech is tinged; thereafter he drops
   all Scotticisms . . . None of the other Scottish characters is distinctly
   nationalized, and there is nothing further that could be taken as intended for typically Scottish about Bohan or Sir Bartram.'

BOHAN
The de'il thou art, whay thou lookest not so big as the king
of Clubs, nor so sharp as the king of Spades, nor so fain as
the king a' Daymonds, be the mass ay take thee to be the
king of false Hearts: therefore I rid thee away, or ay's so   20
curry your kingdom, that you's be glad to run to save your
life.

OBERON
Why stoical Scot, do what thou darest to me, here is my
breast, strike.

BOHAN
Thou wilt not threap me, this whinyard has garred many   25
better men to lope than thou: [*Tries to draw his sword*]
but how now? Gos sayds, what wilt not out? Whay thou
witch, thou de'il, gad's fute, may whinyard.

OBERON
Why, pull man: but what an 'twere out, how then?

BOHAN
This then, thou wert best begone first: for ay'll so lop thy   30
limbs, that thou's go with half a knave's carcase to the de'il.

OBERON
Draw it out, [BOHAN *draws his sword*] now strike fool, can'st
thou not?

BOHAN
Bread ay gad, what de'il is in me, whay tell me thou skipjack,
what art thou?   35

19 *a'Daymonds* ed. (Q Adaymonds)
20 *rid* rede, advise
21 *curry* beat
   kingdom body
23 *stoical* austere
25 *threap* outface
   garred compelled
27 *Gos sayds* God's sides
28 *witch* magician
34 *skipjack* whipper-snapper

---

25 *whinyard.* Short sword (whinyards are referred to as Scottish weapons
   in *Club Law* (c. 1599), V. ii, and *King Edward III* (1595), sig. B2.)
34 *Bread ay gad.* See Bartley, *op. cit.*, p. 82: ' "By the bread of God" is
   found in varying forms in . . . *James IV*; *Vowbreaker*, II. i; *Thierry
   and Theodoret*, V. i; *Scots Figgaries*, I. *James IV* has "by the mary
   masse" and "by the mes" (or "messe") occurs in *Henry V*, *Edward IV*
   and *Club Law*. These seem to be thought characteristic [of Scottish
   speech].'

OBERON

Nay first tell me what thou wast from thy birth, what thou hast passed hitherto, why thou dwellest in a tomb, and leavest the world. And then I will release thee of these bonds, before, not.

BOHAN

And not before, then needs must needs sall: I was born a   40
gentleman of the best blood in all Scotland, except the king; when time brought me to age, and death took my parents, I became a courtier, where though ay list not praise myself, ay engraved the memory of Bohan on the skin-coat of some of them, and revelled with the proudest.   45

OBERON

But why living in such reputation, didst thou leave to be a courtier?

BOHAN

Because my pride was vanity, my expense loss, my reward fair words and large promises, and my hopes spilt, for that after many years' service, one outran me, and what the   50
de'il should I then do there. No, no, flattering knaves that can cog and prate fastest, speed best in the court.

OBERON

To what life didst thou then betake thee?

BOHAN

I then changed the court for the country, and the wars for a wife: but I found the craft of swains more vile, than the   55
knavery of courtiers: the charge of children more heavy than servants, and wives' tongues worse than the wars itself: and therefore I gave o'er that, and went to the city to dwell, and there I kept a great house with small cheer, but all was ne'er the near.   60

OBERON

And why?

BOHAN

Because in seeking friends, I found table guests to eat me and my meat, my wife's gossips to bewray the secrets of my heart, kindred to betray the effect of my life; which when I

44 *skin-coat* skin
52 *cog* flatter, wheedle
   speed prosper, succeed
56 *charge* expense
60 *ne'er the near* never the nearer (to his goal)
63 *bewray* divulge

noted, the court ill, the country worse, and the city worst of   65
all, in good time my wife died: ay would she had died
twenty winter sooner by the mass; leaving my two sons to
the world, and shutting myself into this tomb, where if I die,
I am sure I am safe from wild beasts, but whilst I live,
cannot be free from ill company. Besides, now I am sure gif   70
all my friends fail me, I sall have a grave of mine own
providing: this is all. Now what art thou?

OBERON

Oberon King of Fairies, that loves thee because thou hatest
the world, and to gratulate thee, I brought those antics to
show thee some sport in dancing, which thou hast loved   75
well.

BOHAN

Ha, ha, ha, thinkest thou those puppets can please me?
Whay I have two sons, that with one Scottish jig shall break
the neck of thy antics.

OBERON

That would I fain see.   80

BOHAN

Why thou shalt, ho boys.

Enter SLIPPER *and* NANO

Haud your clacks lads, trattle not for thy life, but gather up
your legs and dance me forthwith a jig worth the sight.

SLIPPER

Why I must talk, on I die for't, wherefore was my tongue
made.   85

BOHAN

Prattle an thou darest ene word more, and ay's dab this
whinyard in thy wemb.

68 *and shutting* some words seem to be missing here
70 *gif* if (Scottish)
74 *gratulate* please, gratify (earliest instance of this sense cited by
   OED)
82 *haud your clacks* hold your tongues (earliest instance of *clacks* in
   this sense cited by *OED*)
   trattle chatter
86 *ene* one
87 *wemb* womb, belly (*OED* does not record this spelling)

73–74 *gif . . . providing.* Cf. *Much Ado*, V. ii, 78: 'If a man do not erect
   in this age his own tomb ere he dies, he shall live no longer in monument
   than the bell rings and the widow weeps.'

OBERON

Be quiet Bohan, I'll strike him dumb, and his brother too,
their talk shall not hinder our jig, fall to it, dance I say man.

BOHAN

Dance Humer, dance, ay rid thee.   90

The two dance a jig devised for the nonce

Now get you to the wide world with more than my father
gave me, that's learning enough, both kinds, knavery and
honesty: and that I gave you, spend at pleasure.

OBERON

Nay, for their sport I will give them this gift, to the dwarf
I give a quick wit, pretty of body, and awarrant his pre-   95
ferment to a prince's service, where by his wisdom he shall
gain more love than common. And to loggerhead your son,
I give a wandering life, and promise he shall never lack:
and avow that if in all distresses he call upon me, to help
him: now let them go.   100

Exeunt with curtsies

BOHAN

Now king, if thou be a king, I will show thee whay I hate
the world, by demonstration. In the year 1520 was in
Scotland, a king overruled with parasites, misled by lust,
and many circumstances too long to trattle on now, much
like our court of Scotland this day; that story have I set   105
down; gang with me to the gallery, and I'll show thee the

---

95 *pretty* prettiness (not recorded by *OED*)   *awarrant* guarantee
97 *loggerhead* block-head   100 s.d. *curtsies* bows

---

88 *I'll . . . dumb.* Cf. *Friar Bacon and Friar Bungay*, 767–778, where Bacon
strikes Bungay dumb to prevent the marriage of Margaret and Lacy.
90 *Humer.* I take *Humer* to be a Scottified form of *humour* (*OED* II 6 b).
102–103 *the year . . . lust.* This cannot refer to James IV, who was killed in
the battle of Flodden, 1513. Ruth Hudson, in 'Greene's *James IV* and
Contemporary Allusions to Scotland', *PMLA* xlvii (1932), 652–667,
argues that 'details in the play bear striking resemblances to actual
events in Scotland in 1590' and that Greene presents 'through his
emphasis on the Scottish king's conceit and susceptibility to flattery . . .
a satire upon the character of James VI'. (pp. 666–667) See lines 104–
105: 'much like our court of Scotland this day'.
106 *the gallery.* Presumably above the inner stage; cf. I. Chorus, 14, *our
harbour*, and II. Chorus, 16, *our cell.* See note to 1 s.d. above, and
R. Hosley, 'The Gallery over the Stage in the Public Playhouse of
Shakespeare's Time', *Shakespeare Quarterly* viii (1957), 15–31, and A. B.
Weiner, 'Elizabethan Interior and Aloft Scenes: A Speculative Essay',
Theatre Survey II (1961), 15–34.

same in action, by guid fellows of our countrymen, and then
when thou seest that, judge if any wise man would not leave
the world if he could.

OBERON

That will I see, lead and I'll follow thee.

110

Exeunt

[Act I, Scene i]

Actus Primus . . . Scena Prima

Laus Deo detur in Æternum

Enter the KING OF ENGLAND, *the* KING OF SCOTS, DOROTHEA *his
Queen, the* COUNTESS, LADY IDA, *with other Lords. And* ATEUKIN
with them aloof

KING OF SCOTS

Brother of England, since our neighbouring land,
And near alliance doth invite our loves,
The more I think upon our last accord,
The more I grieve your sudden parting hence:
First laws of friendship did confirm our peace,   5
Now both the seal of faith and marriage bed,
The name of father, and the style of friend,
These force in me affection full confirmed,
So that I grieve, and this my hearty grief
The heavens record, the world may witness well,   10
To lose your presence, who are now to me
A father, brother, and a vowed friend.

KING OF ENGLAND

Link all these lovely styles good king in one,
And since thy grief exceeds in my depart,
I leave my Dorothea to enjoy   15
Thy whole compact loves, and plighted vows.
Brother of Scotland, this is my joy, my life,
Her father's honour, and her country's hope,
Her mother's comfort, and her husband's bliss:
I tell thee king, in loving of my Doll,   20

7 *style* distinguishing title
15–16 . . . *enjoy/Thy* . . . (Q . . . compact/Loves . . .)

---

s.d. *Laus . . . Æternum.* Let praise be given to God for ever. None of the
    eds. comments; I take the Latin to be the first line or title of an un-
    identified hymn such as the Te Deum.

Thou bind'st her father's heart and all his friends
In bands of love that death cannot dissolve.

KING OF SCOTS

Nor can her father love her like to me,
My life's light, and the comfort of my soul:
Fair Dorothea, that wast England's pride,   25
Welcome to Scotland, and in sign of love,
Lo I invest thee with the Scottish crown.
Nobles and ladies, stoop unto your Queen,
And trumpets sound, that heralds may proclaim
Fair Dorothea peerless Queen of Scots.   30

ALL

Long live and prosper our fair Queen of Scots.

Install and crown her

DOROTHEA

Thanks to the king of kings for my dignity,
Thanks to my father, that provides so carefully,
Thanks to my lord and husband for this honour,
And thanks to all that love their king and me.   35

ALL

Long live fair Dorothea our true queen.

KING OF ENGLAND

Long shine the sun of Scotland in her pride,
Her father's comfort, and fair Scotland's bride.
But Dorothea, since I must depart,
And leave thee from thy tender mother's charge,   40
Let me advise my lovely daughter first,
What best befits her in a foreign land.
Live Doll, for many eyes shall look on thee,
With care of honour and the present state:
For she that steps to height of majesty,   45
Is even the mark whereat the enemy aims.
Thy virtues shall be construed to vice,
Thine affable discourse to abject mind.
If coy, detracting tongues will call thee proud:
Be therefore wary in this slippery state,   50
Honour thy husband, love him as thy life:
Make choice of friends, as eagles of their young,
Who soothe no vice, who flatter not for gain:
But love such friends as do the truth maintain.
Think on these lessons when thou art alone,   55
And thou shalt live in health when I am gone.

44 *With* ed. (Q Haue)

DOROTHEA

   I will engrave these precepts in my heart,
   And as the wind with calmness wooes you hence,
   Even so I wish the heavens in all mishaps,
   May bless my father with continual grace.   60

KING OF ENGLAND

   Then son farewell,
   The favouring winds invites us to depart.
   Long circumstance in taking princely leaves,
   Is more officious than convenient.
   Brother of Scotland, love me in my child,   65
   You greet me well, if so you will her good.

KING OF SCOTS

   Then lovely Doll, and all that favour me,
   Attend to see our English friends at sea,
   Let all their charge depend upon my purse:
   They are our neighbours, by whose kind accord,   70
   We dare attempt the proudest potentate.
   Only fair countess, and your daughter stay,
   With you I have some other thing to say.

       Exeunt all save the KING, *the* COUNTESS, IDA, ATEUKIN,
                              in all royalty

KING OF SCOTS

   [*Aside*] So let them triumph that have cause to joy,
   But wretched king, thy nuptial knot is death,   75
   Thy bride the breeder of thy country's ill,
   For thy false heart dissenting from thy hand,
   Misled by love, hast made another choice,
   Another choice, even when thou vowed'st thy soul
   To Dorothea, England's choicest pride,   80
   O then thy wandering eyes bewitched thy heart,
   Even in the chapel did thy fancy change,
   When, perjured man, though fair Doll had thy hand,
   The Scottish Ida's beauty stale thy heart:
   Yet fear and love hath tied thy ready tongue   85
   From blabbing forth the passions of thy mind,
   Lest fearful silence have in subtle looks

61–62 One line in Q
66 *greet* please (earliest instance cited by *OED*)   *will* intend
69 *charge* expense   84 *stale* stole

---

62 *invites.* The third person plural in -s is frequent in Elizabethan writing
   and occurs several times in *James IV*; see *Abbott*, par. 333. This ed.
   retains the form without noting every instance.

Bewrayed the treason of my new vowed love.
Be fair and lovely Doll, but here's the prize
That lodgeth here, and entered through mine eyes,   90
Yet howso'er I love, I must be wise.
—Now lovely countess, what reward or grace,
May I employ on you for this your zeal,
And humble honours done us in our court,
In entertainment of the English king?   95

COUNTESS
It was of duty prince that I have done:
And what in favour may content me most,
Is, that it please your grace to give me leave,
For to return unto my country home.

KING OF SCOTS
But lovely Ida is your mind the same?   100

IDA
I count of court my lord, as wise men do,
'Tis fit for those that knows what 'longs thereto:
Each person to his place, the wise to art,
The cobbler to his clout, the swain to cart.

KING OF SCOTS
But Ida you are fair, and beauty shines,   105
And seemeth best, where pomp her pride refines.

IDA
If beauty (as I know there's none in me)
Were sworn my love, and I his life should be,
The farther from the court I were removed,
The more I think of heaven I were beloved.   110

KING OF SCOTS
And why?

IDA
Because the court is counted Venus' net,
Where gifts and vows for stales are often set,
None, be she chaste as Vesta, but shall meet
A curious tongue to charm her ears with sweet.   115

KING OF SCOTS
Why Ida then I see you set at naught
The force of love.

93 *employ on* bestow on
104 *clout* piece of leather for shoe-making or mending
113 *stales* lures, bait
115 *curious* expert, skilful
    sweet pleasure
117–118 . . . *thought/Most* . . . (Q . . . king,/That . . .)

IDA   In sooth this is my thought
 Most gracious king, that they that little prove
 Are mickle blest, from bitter sweets of love:
 And weel I wot, I heard a shepherd sing,   120
 That like a bee, Love hath a little sting:
 He lurks in flowers, he percheth on the trees,
 He on kings' pillows bends his pretty knees:
 The Boy is blind, but when he will not spy,
 He hath a leaden shot, and wings to fly: 125
 Beshrew me yet, for all these strange effects,
 If I would like the lad, that so infects.
KING OF SCOTS
 [*Aside*] Rare wit, fair face, what heart could more desire?
 But Doll is fair, and doth concern thee near.
 Let Doll be fair, she is won, but I must woo,   130
 And win fair Ida, there's some choice in two.
 —But Ida thou art coy.
IDA   And why dread king?
KING OF SCOTS
 In that you will dispraise so sweet a thing
 As love; had I my wish,
IDA
 What then?
KING OF SCOTS Then would I place   135
 His arrow here, his beauty in that face.
IDA
 And were Apollo moved and ruled by me,
 His wisdom should be yours, and mine his tree.
KING OF SCOTS
 But here returns our train. Welcome fair Doll:
 How fares our father, is he shipped and gone?   140

       Enters the train back

124 *The Boy* Cupid
133–134 . . . *thing*/*As* . . . (Q . . . sweet/A thing . . .)
135–136 . . . *place*/*His* . . . (Q . . . here,/His . . .)
137 *Apollo* god of social and intellectual order
138 *his tree* the laurel tree into which Daphne was turned when
  fleeing from Apollo
139–140 . . . *Doll:*/*How* . . . (Q . . . train./Welcome . . .)
140 *shipped* embarked

---

125 *shot.* All other eds. follow Q in reading *foote* (foot); but Ida is warning
  the king of the dangers of love, and one of them was Cupid's leaden, as
  opposed to his golden, arrow.

DOROTHEA

  My royal father is both shipped and gone,
  God and fair winds direct him to his home.

KING OF SCOTS

  Amen say I, [*Aside*] would thou wert with him too:
  Then might I have a fitter time to woo.
  —But countess you would be gone, therefore farewell,   145
  Yet Ida if thou wilt, stay thou behind,
  To accompany my queen.
  But if thou like the pleasures of the court,
  [*Aside*] Or if she liked me though she left the court,
  What should I say? I know not what to say,   150
  —You may depart, and you my courteous queen,
  Leave me a space, I have a weighty cause
  To think upon: [*Aside*] Ida, it nips me near:
  It came from thence, I feel it burning here.

               Exeunt all saving the KING *and* ATEUKIN

  Now am I free from sight of common eye,   155
  Where to myself I may disclose the grief
  That hath too great a part in mine affects.

ATEUKIN

  [*Aside*] And now is my time, by wiles and words to rise,
  Greater than those, that thinks themselves more wise.

KING OF SCOTS

  And first fond king, thy honour doth engrave   160
  Upon thy brows, the drift of thy disgrace:
  Thy new vowed love in sight of God and men
  Links thee to Dorothea, during life,
  For who more fair and virtuous than thy wife.
  Deceitful murtherer of a quiet mind,   165
  Fond love, vile lust, that thus misleads us men,
  To vow our faiths, and fall to sin again.
  But kings stoop not to every common thought,
  Ida is fair and wise, fit for a king:

148 *But if* on condition that
152–153 . . . *cause*/*To* . . . (Q . . . vpon:/Ida . . .)
153 *nips me near* affects me painfully
154 *It came from thence* (punning allusion to Mt. Ida, a haunt of
     Cupid and Venus)
157 *mine* used interchangeably with *my* in Elizabethan writing; see
     Abbott, par. 237
     affects desires
159 *thinks* Elizabethan third person plural; see *Abbott*, par. 333
163 *Links* ed. (Q Linke)

And for fair Ida will I hazard life,   170
Venture my kingdom, country, and my crown:
Such fire hath love, to burn a kingdom down.
Say Doll dislikes, that I estrange my love,
Am I obedient to a woman's look?
Nay, say her father frown when he shall hear   175
That I do hold fair Ida's love so dear:
Let father frown and fret, and fret and die,
Nor earth, nor heaven shall part my love and I.
Yea they shall part us, but we first must meet,
And woo, and win, and yet the world not see't.   180
Yea there's the wound, and wounded with that thought
So let me die: for all my drift is naught.

ATEUKIN
Most gracious and imperial majesty,
[*Aside*] A little flattery more were but too much,

KING OF SCOTS
Villain what art thou   185
That thus darest interrupt a prince's secrets.

ATEUKIN
Dread king, thy vassal is a man of art,
Who knows by constellation of the stars,
By oppositions and by dire aspects,
The things are past, and those that are to come.   190

KING OF SCOTS
But where's thy warrant to approach my presence?

ATEUKIN
My zeal and ruth to see your grace's wrong,
Makes me lament, I did detract so long.

KING OF SCOTS
If thou know'st thoughts, tell me what mean I now?

ATEUKIN
I'll calculate the cause   195
Of those your highness' smiles, and tell your thoughts.

184 Q assigns to King of Scots
185–186 One line in Q
189 *dire* ed. (Q drie)
192 *ruth* pity   193 *detract* delay
195–196 . . . *cause/Of* . . . (Q . . . smiles,/And . . .)

189 *oppositions*. Occasions when two heavenly bodies are exactly opposite
  each other as seen from the earth's surface.
  dire aspects. Relative positions of the heavenly bodies considered malign
  by astrologers.

KING OF SCOTS
> But lest thou spend thy time in idleness,
> And miss the matter that my mind aims at,
> Tell me,

He strikes him on the ear

> What star was opposite when that was thought?   200

ATEUKIN
> 'Tis inconvenient mighty potentate,
> Whose looks resembles Jove in majesty,
> To scorn the sooth of science with contempt;
> I see in those imperial looks of yours,
> The whole discourse of love; Saturn combust,   205
> With direful looks, at your nativity
> Beheld fair Venus in her silver orb.
> I know by certain axioms I have read,
> Your grace's griefs, and further can express
> Her name, that holds you thus in fancy's bands.   210

KING OF SCOTS
> Thou talkest wonders.

ATEUKIN   Naught but truth O king,
> 'Tis Ida is the mistress of your heart,
> Whose youth must take impression of affects,
> For tender twigs will bow, and milder minds
> Will yield to fancy, be they followed well.   215

KING OF SCOTS
> What god art thou composed in human shape,
> Or bold Trophonius to decide our doubts,
> How know'st thou this?

199, 200 One line in Q, s.d. following
201 *inconvenient* unreasonable   203 *sooth* truth, facts
205 *combust* within 8½ degrees of the sun
208 *axioms* astrological principles
209–210 . . . *express*/*Her* . . . (Q . . . name,/That . . .)
215 *fancy* amorous inclination
216 *composed* framed
217 *Trophonius* an oracle at Lebadea in Boeotia

205–207 *Saturn . . . With direful looks . . . Beheld . . . Venus.* The planets were aspecting one another either in quadrat (90 degrees apart) or opposition (180 degrees apart), both malefic aspects in astrology (see Johnstone Parr, 'Ateukin the Astrologer in Robert Greene's *James the Fourth*', in *Tamburlaine's Malady*, 1953, p. 52). Parr remarks: 'But Ateukin persuades James to believe that the configuration means precisely the opposite of what it does mean: for the quadrat aspect between Sol and Venus means that James shall not possess Ida' (p. 53).

ATEUKIN   Even as I know the means
   To work your grace's freedom and your love:
   Had I the mind as many courtiers have,   220
   To creep into your bosom for your coin,
   And beg rewards for every cap and knee,
   I then would say, if that your grace would give
   This lease, this manor, or this patent sealed,
   For this or that I would effect your love: 225
   But Ateukin is no parasite O prince,
   I know your grace knows scholars are but poor,
   And therefore as I blush to beg a fee,
   Your mightiness is so magnificent
   You cannot choose but cast some gift apart,   230
   To ease my bashful need that cannot beg.
   As for your love, oh might I be employed,
   How faithfully would Ateukin compass it:
   But princes rather trust a smoothing tongue,
   Than men of art that can accept the time.   235

KING OF SCOTS
   Ateukin, if so thy name, for so thou say'st,
   Thine art appears in entrance of my love:
   And since I deem thy wisdom matched with truth,
   I will exalt thee, and thyself alone
   Shalt be the agent to dissolve my grief.   240
   Sooth is, I love, and Ida is my love,
   But my new marriage nips me near, Ateukin,
   For Dorothea may not brook th'abuse.

ATEUKIN
   These lets are but as motes against the sun,
   Yet not so great, like dust before the wind: 245
   Yet not so light. Tut, pacify your grace,
   You have the sword and sceptre in your hand,
   You are the king, the state depends on you:
   Your will is law, say that the case were mine,

222 *cap and knee* salute and bow
235 *accept the time* undertake the responsibility
244 *motes* ed. (Q moaths)

---

244 *motes.* Cf. *Love's Labour's Lost*, IV. iii, 159: 'You found his mote; the
king your mote did see,' where the quartos and folios spell the word
moth. There is constant confusion between *moth* and *mote*, cf. *Othello*,
I. iii, 257; *Pericles*, IV. iv, 21; *King John*, IV. i, 92. Apparently they
were often used synonymously and spelled haphazardly. *Mote* in the
modern sense was spelled *moth*, as in the old editions of *Love's Labour's
Lost*, and *moth* seems to have been pronounced mote.

Were she my sister whom your highness loves, 250
She should consent, for that our lives, our goods,
Depend on you, and if your queen repine,
Although my nature cannot brook of blood,
And scholars grieve to hear of murtherous deeds,
But if the lamb should let the lion's way, 255
By my advice the lamb should lose her life.
Thus am I bold to speak unto your grace,
Who am too base to kiss your royal feet,
For I am poor, nor have I land nor rent,
Nor countenance here in court, but for my love, 260
Your grace shall find none such within the realm.

KING OF SCOTS
Wilt thou effect my love, shall she be mine?

ATEUKIN
I'll gather moly, crocus, and the herbs
That heals the wounds of body and the mind,
I'll set out charms and spells, naught else shall be left, 265
To tame the wanton if she shall rebel,
Give me but tokens of your highness' trust.

KING OF SCOTS
Thou shalt have gold, honour and wealth enough,
Win my love, and I will make thee great.

ATEUKIN
These words do make me rich most noble prince, 270
I am more proud of them than any wealth,
Did not your grace suppose I flatter you,
Believe me I would boldly publish this:
Was never eye that saw a sweeter face,
Nor never ear that heard a deeper wit, 275
O God how I am ravished in your worth.

KING OF SCOTS
Ateukin follow me, love must have ease.

ATEUKIN
I'll kiss your highness' feet, march when you please.

Exeunt

255 *But* yet 260 *countenance* patronage
263 *moly, crocus* ed. (Q Moly-rocus) 273 *publish* report publicly

268 *Thou . . . gold.* Cf. the similar promise in a similar situation in *Apius and Virginia*, 463–470:
  And friend, I sweare by Iubiter, and eke by Iuno's seate:
  And else by all the misteries, where on thou canst intreate
  Thou shalt possesse and haue, I will thee graunt and geue,
  The greatest part of all my Realme, for aye thee to releeue.

[Act I, Scene ii]

Enter SLIPPER, NANO, *and* ANDREW, *with their bills ready written in their hands*

ANDREW
　Stand back sir, mine shall stand highest.
SLIPPER
　Come under mine arm sir, or get a footstool, or else by the
　light of the moon, I must come to it.
NANO
　Agree my masters, every man to his height, though I stand
　lowest, I hope to get the best master.　　　　　　　　　5
ANDREW
　Ere I will stoop to a thistle, I will change turns, as good luck
　comes on the right hand, as the left: here's for me,
SLIPPER
　And me,
NANO
　And mine.　　　　　　　　　　　[*They put up bills*]
ANDREW
　But tell me fellows till better occasion come, do you seek　　10
　masters?
BOTH
　We do.
ANDREW
　But what can you do worthy preferment?
NANO
　Marry I can smell a knave from a rat.
SLIPPER
　And I can lick a dish before a cat.　　　　　　　　15
ANDREW
　And I can find two fools unsought, how like you that? But in
　earnest, now tell me of what trades are you two?
SLIPPER
　How mean you that sir, of what trade? Marry I'll tell you,

s.d. *bills* posters, advertisements
　　Q prints this scene as verse, though clearly 1–40 and 70–139 is
　　prose　　　　6–11 Q assigns to Andrew
　6 *change turns* change direction
　12 s.p. BOTH ed. (Q Ambo)

　6 *Ere . . . thistle.* Perhaps an allusion to the proverb 'They have need of a
　blessing that kneel to a thistle' (*Tilley* N 83).

I have many trades, the honest trade when I needs must,
the filching trade when time serves, the cozening trade as I   20
find occasion. And I have more qualities, I cannot abide a
full cup unkissed, a fat capon uncarved, a full purse
unpicked, nor a fool to prove a Justice as you do.

ANDREW
Why sot, why call'st thou me fool?

NANO
For examining wiser than thyself.   25

ANDREW
So doth many more than I in Scotland.

NANO
Yea those are such, as have more authority than wit, and
more wealth than honesty.

SLIPPER
This is my little brother with the great wit, 'ware him.
But what canst thou do, tell me, that art so inquisitive of us?   30

ANDREW
Any thing that concerns a gentleman to do, that can I do.

SLIPPER
So you are of the gentle trade?

ANDREW
True.

SLIPPER
Then gentle sir, leave us to our selves, for here comes one as
if he would lack a servant ere he went.   35

Enter ATEUKIN

ATEUKIN
Why so Ateukin? This becomes thee best,
Wealth, honour, ease, and angels in thy chest:
Now may I say, as many often sing,
No fishing to the sea, nor service to a king.
Unto this high promotion doth belong   40
Means to be talked of in the thickest throng:
And first to fit the humours of my lord,
Sweet lays and lines of love I must record.
And such sweet lines and love-lays I'll indite

---

32 *the gentle trade* shoemaking (*OED*'s earliest example is from
   George-a-Greene [1592])
34–35 *as if . . . went* i.e., hire a new one and dismiss an old
37 *angels* gold coins each worth ten shillings
39 *No fishing . . . king* cf. *Tilley* F 336
40 *promotion* ed. (Q promotions)

As men may wish for, and my liege delight,   45
And next a train of gallants at my heels,
That men may say, the world doth run on wheels.
For men of art, that rise by indirection,
To honour and the favour of their king,
Must use all means to save what they have got,   50
And win their favours whom he never knew.
If any frown to see my fortunes such,
A man must bear a little, not too much:
But in good time: these bills portend, I think,
That some good fellows do for service seek.   55

Read

*If any gentleman, spiritual or temporal, will entertain out of
his service, a young stripling of the age of thirty years, that
can sleep with the soundest, eat with the hungriest, work with
the sickest, lie with the loudest, face with the proudest, etc., that
can wait in a gentleman's chamber, when his master is a mile off,*   60
*keep his stable when 'tis empty, and his purse when 'tis full, and
hath many qualities worse than all these, let him write his name
and go his way, and attendance shall be given.*
By my faith, a good servant, which is he?
SLIPPER
Truly sir, that am I.   65
ATEUKIN
And why dost thou write such a bill, are all these qualities
in thee?
SLIPPER
O Lord aye sir, and a great many more, some better, some
worse, some richer, some poorer, why sir do you look so, do
they not please you?   70
ATEUKIN
Truly no, for they are naught and so art thou. If thou hast
no better qualities, stand by.
SLIPPER
O sir, I tell the worst first, but and you lack a man, I am for
you, I'll tell you the best qualities I have.
ATEUKIN
Be brief then.   75
SLIPPER
If you need me in your chamber, I can keep the door at a

56–63 'The humour lies in the representation of disqualifications as
qualifications.' (Collins.)

whistle, in your kitchen, turn the spit, and lick the pan,
and make the fire burn. But if in the stable,

ATEUKIN
Yea there would I use thee.

SLIPPER
Why there you kill me, there am I, and turn me to a horse   80
and a wench, and I have no peer.

ATEUKIN
Art thou so good in keeping a horse, I pray thee tell me
how many good qualities hath a horse?

SLIPPER
Why so sir, a horse hath two properties of a man, that is, a
proud heart, and a hardy stomach, four properties of a lion,   85
a broad breast, a stiff docket, hold your nose master, a wild
countenance, and four good legs. Nine properties of a fox,
nine of a hare, nine of an ass, and ten of a woman.

ATEUKIN
A woman, why what properties of a woman hath a horse?

SLIPPER
O master, know you not that? Draw your tables, and write   90
what wise I speak. First, a merry countenance. Second, a
soft pace. Third, a broad forehead. Fourth, broad buttocks.
Fifth, hard of ward. Sixth, easy to leap upon. Seventh, good
at long journey. Eighth, well moving under a man. Ninth,
always busy with the mouth. Tenth, ever chewing on the   95
bridle.

80 *there am I* I am at hand (*OED there* B IV 12 a)
    and turn me to put me to work to (*OED* VIII 79 b; earliest
    example 1840)
86 *docket* the solid fleshy part of an animal's tail (?) *OED* cites as
    unique example
90 *tables* writing-tablet
94 *well moving* ed. (Q *mouing*)

---

77 *lick the pan.* Lie, flatter, be a parasite. Slipper is probably being deliber-
    ately ambiguous here.
80 *there you kill me.* Have me exactly (?) This slang use is not recorded in
    any dictionary consulted, but cf. III. i, 47: 'I am dead at . . .'.
93 *hard of ward.* Hard to control (?) The immediate context suggests a
    double entendre, perhaps playing on *ward* (*OED* VI 24 a, the inside of
    a lock)
94 *well moving.* Collins was the first editor to point to Fitzherbert's *Book of
    Husbandry* (which Greene follows almost verbatim) as the source of
    lines 91–96. Fitzherbert reads: 'viii. to be well sturryng vnder a man'.
    Without the word *well* the point is lost.

ATEUKIN
Thou art a man for me, what's thy name?
SLIPPER
An ancient name sir, belonging to the chamber and the
night-gown. Guess you that.
ATEUKIN
What's that, Slipper?   100
SLIPPER
By my faith well guessed, and so 'tis indeed: you'll be my
master?
ATEUKIN
I mean so.
SLIPPER
Read this first.
ATEUKIN
Pleaseth it any gentleman to entertain a servant of more wit   105
than stature, let them subscribe, and attendance shall be given.
What of this?
SLIPPER
He is my brother sir, and we two were born together, must
serve together, and will die together, though we be both
hanged.   110
ATEUKIN
What's thy name?
NANO
Nano.
ATEUKIN
The etymology of which word is, a dwarf: art not thou the
old stoic's son that dwells in his tomb?
BOTH
We are.   115
ATEUKIN
Thou art welcome to me, wilt thou give thyself wholly to be
at my disposition?
NANO
In all humility I submit myself.
ATEUKIN
Then will I deck thee princely, instruct thee courtly, and
present thee to the queen as my gift. Art thou content?   120

115 s.p. BOTH ed. (Q Ambo)

---

113 *The etymology . . . dwarf.* Ateukin is correct; the name is derived from
    Latin *nanus*, a dwarf.

NANO

Yes, and thank your honour too.

SLIPPER

Then welcome brother, and fellow now.

ANDREW

May it please your honour to abase your eye so low, as to
look either on my bill or myself.

ATEUKIN

What are you?   125

ANDREW

By birth a gentleman, in profession a scholar, and one that
knew your honour in Edinburgh, before your worthiness
called you to this reputation, by name Andrew Snoord.

ATEUKIN

Andrew I remember thee, follow me, and we will confer
further, for my weighty affairs for the king, commands me to   130
be brief at this time. Come on Nano, Slipper follow.

Exeunt

[Act I, Scene iii]

Enter SIR BARTRAM *with* EUSTACE *and others, booted*

SIR BARTRAM

But tell me lovely Eustace as thou lov'st me,
Among the many pleasures we have passed,
Which is the rifest in thy memory,
To draw thee over to thine ancient friend?

EUSTACE

What makes Sir Bartram thus inquisitive?   5
Tell me good knight, am I welcome or no?

SIR BARTRAM

By sweet Saint Andrew and may sale I swear,
As welcome is my honest Dick to me,
As morning's sun, or as the watery moon,
In merkist night, when we the borders track.   10
I tell thee Dick, thy sight hath cleared my thoughts
Of many baneful troubles that there woond.
Welcome to Sir Bartram as his life:
Tell me bonny Dick, hast got a wife?

128 *by name* ed. (Q by me)
  1 *lovely* friendly
  3 *rifest* most recurrent
  7 *may sale* my soul
 10 *merkist* darkest   12 *woond* wound

EUSTACE

A wife? God shield Sir Bartram, that were ill   15
To leave my wife and wander thus astray:
But time and good advice ere many years,
May chance to make my fancy bend that way.
What news in Scotland? Therefore came I hither:
To see your country, and to chat together.   20

SIR BARTRAM

Why man, our country's blithe, our king is well,
Our queen so, so, the nobles well, and worse,
And weel are they that were about the king,
But better are the country gentlemen.
And I may tell thee Eustace, in our lives,   25
We old men never saw so wondrous change:
But leave this trattle, and tell me what news,
In lovely England with our honest friends?

EUSTACE

The king, the court, and all our noble friends
Are well, and God in mercy keep them so.   30
The northern lords and ladies hereabouts,
That knows I came to see your queen and court,
Commends them to my honest friend Sir Bartram,
And many others that I have not seen:
Among the rest, the Countess Elinor,   35
From Carlisle where we merry oft have been,
Greets well my lord, and hath directed me,
By message, this fair lady's face to see.

[Shows a portrait]

SIR BARTRAM

I tell thee Eustace, lest mine old eyes daze,
This is our Scottish moon and evening's pride: 40
This is the blemish of your English bride:
Who sails by her, are sure of wind at will.

23 *weel* well
27 *trattle* chatter; cf. Induction, 85
35–36 . . . *Elinor,/From* . . . (Q . . . Carlile/Where . . .)

---

23 *were.* As the next line shows, things are not as well as Sir Bartram
   pretends. The king has probably already driven away some of his
   nobles before his dismissal of Douglas, Morton, and the Bishop of St.
   Andrews (II. ii, 112 ff.).
42 *are . . . will.* Are sure to have conditions or circumstances favourable
   to their purpose (*OED wind* III 15 b). But the context suggests the
   reverse (storm); see 43.

Her face is dangerous, her sight is ill:
And yet in sooth sweet Dick, it may be said,
The king hath folly, there's virtue in the maid.   45
EUSTACE
But knows my friend this portrait, be advised?
SIR BARTRAM
Is it not Ida the Countess of Arran's daughter's?
EUSTACE
So was I told by Elinor of Carlisle,
But tell me lovely Bartram, is the maid
Evil inclined, misled, or concubine   50
Unto the king or any other lord?
SIR BARTRAM
Should I be brief and true, then thus my Dick,
All England's grounds yields not a blither lass,
Nor Europe can surpass her for her gifts,
Of virtue, honour, beauty, and the rest: 55
But our fond king not knowing sin in lust,
Makes love by endless means and precious gifts,
And men that see it dare not say't my friend,
But we may wish that it were otherwise:
But I rid thee to view the picture still,   60
For by the person's sights there hangs some ill.
EUSTACE
Oh good Sir Bartram, you suspect I love,
Then were I mad, she whom I never saw,
But howso'er, I fear not enticings,
Desire will give no place unto a king: 65
I'll see her whom the world admires so much,
That I may say with them, there lives none such.
SIR BARTRAM
Be Gad and sall, both see and talk with her,

49–51 ... *maid*/*Evil* ... *concubine*/*Unto* ... (Q ... inclind,/Mis-
    led ... Lord?)
54 *surpass* ed. (Q art)
60 *rid* rede, advise
61 *sights* glances
62–67 Q assigns to Sir Bartram
63 *she* (Q hee) cf. reverse error at II. i, 131, and *Abbott*, par. 211 '*she*
    for *her*'

60–61 *But ... ill.* 'I advise you to keep looking at the picture; it is safer
    than exposing yourself to the glances of the person herself'.
61 Cf. Middleton and Rowley, *The Changeling*, II. i, 36: 'As if danger
    or ill luck hung in my looks.'

And when th'hast done, whate'er her beauty be,
I'll warrant thee her virtues may compare,   70
With the proudest she that waits upon your queen.

[Enter SERVANT]

SERVANT
My lady entreats your worship in to supper.

SIR BARTRAM
Guid bonny Dick, my wife will tell thee more,
Was never no man in her book before:
Be Gad she's blithe, fair, lewely, bonny, etc.   *Exeunt* 75

[Chorus]

Enter BOHAN *and the fairy king after the first act, to them a
round of fairies, or some pretty dance*

BOHAN
Be Gad, gramercies little king for this,
This sport is better in my exile life,
Than ever the deceitfuil werld could yield.

OBERON
I tell thee Bohan, Oberon is king,
Of quiet, pleasure, profit, and content,   5
Of wealth, of honour, and of all the world,

72 Q assigns to Eustace
75 *lewely* Scottified form of *lovely*
s.d. *a round* a dance in which the performers circle
 1 *gramercies* thanks

---

74 *in her book.* In her favour; cf. 'to be in someone's good or bad books';
   OED does not specifically record the sense of 'romantic attachment'
   that the phrase carries here.
75 *etc.* Dyce asks: 'Was the player here to speak extempore whatever he
   chose?' Grosart comments: 'Rather = goes out talking.'
 1 *little king.* White Latham in *The Elizabethan Fairies* (1931) argues that
   the small size of the later English fairies is a result of Shakespeare's
   invention, adopted immediately by other writers, and passing into
   folklore, but K. M. Briggs, *The Anatomy of Puck* (1959), points out that
   'The ordinary fairy people of Britain dwindle down from these heroic
   fairies . . . some are the size of a three-years' child, like Oberon in
   Huon of Bordeaux, some . . . are three spans in height. . . . Their size
   seems naturally small' (pp. 14–15). Greene here seems to be following
   the lead of John Lyly, who had introduced fairies into *Endimion* (published 1591), *Gallathea*, and *The Maydes Metamorphosis*, 'probably . . .
   to fit in dances for the smaller children,' (Briggs, p. 48).

Tied to no place, yet all are tied to me.
Live thou in this life, exiled from world and men,
And I will show thee wonders ere we part.
BOHAN
Then mark my stay, and the strange doubts,   10
That follow flatterers, lust and lawless will,
And then say I have reason to forsake
The world, and all that are within the same.
Go shroud us in our harbour where we'll see
The pride of folly, as it ought to be.   15

                                                    Exeunt

[Act II, Scene i]

Actus Secundus . . . Scena Prima

Enter the COUNTESS OF ARRAN, *with* IDA *her daughter in their
porch, sitting at work*
A song

COUNTESS
Fair Ida, might you choose the greatest good
Midst all the world, in blessings that abound,
Wherein my daughter should your liking be?
IDA
Not in delights, or pomp, or majesty.
COUNTESS
And why?
IDA   Since these are means to draw the mind   5
From perfect good, and make true judgement blind.
COUNTESS
Might you have wealth, and fortune's richest store?
IDA
Yet would I (might I choose) be honest poor.
For she that sits at fortune's feet a-low
Is sure she shall not taste a further woe.   10

7 *me* ed. (Q one)
9 *wonders* ed. (Q wonters)
10 *doubts* apprehensions, fears
12–13 . . . *forsake/The* . . . (Q . . . world,/And . . .)

---

7 *me.* The emphasis of the whole speech is on Oberon's personal power,
   and the emendation seems justifiable on that account.
14 *harbour.* Resting-place (not *arbour* as other eds. gloss); cf. Induction,
   106 *the gallery*; II. Chorus, 16 *our cell.*

But those that prank on top of fortune's ball,
Still fear a change: and fearing catch a fall.

COUNTESS

Tut foolish maid, each one contemneth need.

IDA

Good reason why, they know not good indeed.

COUNTESS

Many marry then, on whom distress doth lour,   15

IDA

Yes, they that virtue deem an honest dower.
Madam, by right this world I may compare
Unto my work, wherein with heedful care
The heavenly workman plants with curious hand,
As I with needle draw each thing on land,   20
Even as he list, some men like to the rose,
Are fashioned fresh, some in their stalks do close,
And born do sudden die: some are but weeds,
And yet from them a secret good proceeds:
I with my needle, if I please may blot   25
The fairest rose within my cambric plot,
God with a beck can change each worldly thing,
The poor to rich, the beggar to the king.
What then hath man, wherein he well may boast,
Since by a beck he lives, a lour is lost?   30

Enter EUSTACE *with letters*

COUNTESS

Peace Ida, here are strangers near at hand.

EUSTACE

Madam God speed.

COUNTESS   I thank you gentle squire.

EUSTACE

The country Countess of Northumberland

11 *prank* show off
19 *curious* skilful
20 *draw* depict (in embroidery)
21 *list* wishes
25 *blot* efface, destroy
28 *rich* ed. (Q earth)   30 *lour* frown

---

11 *fortune's ball*. In Renaissance iconography the goddess Fortune was
represented standing on a sphere, symbolizing her fickleness.
28 *rich*. Emendation seems necessary to balance the antithesis of the line.
33 *country . . . Northumberland*. 'Countess having landed property in
Northumberland and residing there' (*OED country* III 16).

Doth greet you well, and hath requested me
To bring these letters to your ladyship.   35

He carries the letters

COUNTESS
I thank her honour, and yourself my friend.

She receives and peruseth them

I see she means you good, brave gentleman,
Daughter, the Lady Elinor salutes
Yourself as well as me, then for her sake
'Twere good you entertained that courtier well.   40
IDA
As much salute as may become my sex,
And he in virtue can vouchsafe to think,
I yield him for the courteous countess' sake.
Good sir sit down, my mother here and I,
Count time misspent an endless vanity.   45
EUSTACE
[*Aside*] Beyond report, the wit, the fair, the shape—
What work you here, fair mistress may I see it?
IDA
Good sir look on, how like you this compact?
EUSTACE
Methinks in this I see true love in act:
The woodbines with their leaves do sweetly spread,   50
The roses blushing prank them in their red,
No flower but boasts the beauties of the spring,
This bird hath life indeed if it could sing:
What means fair mistress had you in this work?
IDA
My needle sir.
EUSTACE   In needles then there lurks   55
Some hidden grace I deem beyond my reach.
IDA
Not grace in them good sir, but those that teach.
EUSTACE
Say that your needle now were Cupid's sting,

35 s.d. *carries* displays
   s.d. *letters* ed. (Q letter)
46 *the fair* the beauty
48 *compact* composition (antedates *OED*'s earliest example from
   1601)
51 *prank them* deck themselves out

[*Aside*] But ah her eye must be no less,
In which is heaven and heavenliness,   60
In which the food of gods is shut,
Whose powers the purest minds do glut.

IDA

What if it were?

EUSTACE   Then see a wondrous thing,
I fear me you would paint in Tereus' heart,
Affection in his power and chiefest part.   65

IDA

Good Lord sir no, for hearts but pricked soft,
Are wounded sore, for so I hear it oft.

EUSTACE

What recks the wound, where but your happy eye,
May make him live, whom Jove hath judged to die.

IDA

Should life and death within this needle lurk,   70
I'll prick no hearts, I'll prick upon my work.

Enter ATEUKIN *with* SLIPPER *the clown*

COUNTESS

Peace Ida, I perceive the fox at hand.

EUSTACE

The fox? Why, fetch your hounds and chase him hence.

COUNTESS

Oh sir these great men bark at small offence.
Come, will it please you to enter gentle sir?   75

Offer to exeunt

ATEUKIN

Stay courteous ladies, favour me so much,
As to discourse a word or two apart.

COUNTESS

Good sir, my daughter learns this rule of me,
To shun resort, and strangers' company:

65 *part* ed. (Q parts)
68 *What . . . eye,* (Q . . . second,/Where . . .)
   wound ed. (Q second)
75 Q assigns to Ateukin
80 *shifting mates* fraudulent fellows

59–62 These lines should be marked as an aside, as the rhyming of lines
   58 and 63 indicates.
64 *Tereus'* ed. (Q Teueus). Tereus was married to Procne. He raped her
   sister Philomela and cut out his victim's tongue (Ovid, *Met.*, *VI*).

For some are shifting mates that carry letters,   80
Some such as you too good, because our betters.
SLIPPER
Now I pray you sir, what akin are you to a pickerel?
ATEUKIN
Why knave?
SLIPPER
By my troth sir, because I never knew a proper situation
fellow of your pitch, fitter to swallow a gudgeon.   85
ATEUKIN
What mean'st thou by this?
SLIPPER
Shifting fellow sir, these be thy words, shifting fellow: this
gentlewoman I fear me, knew your bringing up.
ATEUKIN
How so?
SLIPPER
Why sir your father was a miller, that could shift for a peck of   90
grist in a bushel, and you a fair spoken gentleman, that can
get more land by a lie, than an honest man by his ready
money.
ATEUKIN
Caitiff what sayest thou?
SLIPPER
I say sir, that if she call you shifting knave, you shall not put   95
her to the proof.
ATEUKIN
And why?
SLIPPER
Because sir, living by your wit as you do, shifting is your
letters patents: it were a hard matter for me to get my
dinner that day, wherein my master had not sold a dozen   100
of devices, a case of cogs, and a suit of shifts in the morning:
I speak this in your commendation sir, and I pray you so
take it.

82 *pickerel* young pike
85 *gudgeon* credulous person (literally, a small fish)
87 *thy words* the words which describe, or are applicable to, you
87–96 *this . . . proof* Q prints as verse
101 *devices* plots, tricks   *cogs* deceptions, frauds
     shifts subterfuges

84–85 *situation fellow.* Employed servant (used contemptuously). *OED*'s
earliest example of *situation* in reference to employment is from 1813.

ATEUKIN

    If I live knave I will be revenged, what gentleman would
    entertain a rascal, thus to derogate from his honour?   105

IDA

    My lord why are you thus impatient?

ATEUKIN

    Not angry Ida, but I teach this knave
    How to behave himself among his betters:
    Behold fair countess to assure your stay,
    I here present the signet of the king,   110
    Who now by me fair Ida doth salute you:
    And since in secret I have certain things,
    In his behalf good madam to impart,
    I crave your daughter to discourse apart.

COUNTESS

    She shall in humble duty be addressed,   115
    To do his highness' will in what she may.

IDA

    Now gentle sir what would his grace with me?

ATEUKIN

    Fair comely nymph, the beauty of your face,
    Sufficient to bewitch the heavenly powers,
    Hath wrought so much in him, that now of late   120
    He finds himself made captive unto love,
    And though his power and majesty requires
    A straight command before an humble suit,
    Yet he his mightiness doth so abase,
    As to entreat your favour, honest maid.   125

IDA

    Is he not married sir unto our queen?

ATEUKIN

    He is.

IDA   And are not they by God accurs't,
    That sever them whom he hath knit in one?

ATEUKIN

    They be: what then? We seek not to displace
    The princess from her seat, but since by love   130

122-125 A rhetorical commonplace, cf. *Love's Labour's Lost*, IV. i, 79-80:
    'Shall I command thy love? I may. Shall I enforce thy love? I could.
    Shall I entreat thy love? I will.'; *Hamlet*, II. ii, 27-30:
        Both your majesties
        Might, by the sovereign power you have of us,
        Put your dread pleasures more into command
        Than to entreaty.

The king is made your own, he is resolved
In private to accept your dalliance,
In spite of war, watch, or worldly eye.

IDA

Oh how he talks as if he should not die,
As if that God in justice once could wink,   135
Upon that fault I am ashamed to think.

ATEUKIN

Tut mistress, man at first was born to err,
Women are not all formed to be saints:
'Tis impious for to kill our native king,
Whom by a little favour we may save.   140

IDA

Better than live unchaste, to live in grave.

ATEUKIN

He shall erect your state and wed you well.

IDA

But can his warrant keep my soul from hell?

ATEUKIN

He will enforce, if you resist his suit.

IDA

What though, the world may shame to him account,   145
To be a king of men and worldly pelf,
Yet hath no power to rule and guide himself.

ATEUKIN

I know you gentle lady and the care
Both of your honour and his grace's health
Makes me confused in this dangerous state.   150

IDA

So counsel him, but soothe thou not his sin,
'Tis vain allurement that doth make him love,
I shame to hear, be you ashamed to move.

COUNTESS

I see my daughter grows impatient,
I fear me he pretends some bad intent.   155

ATEUKIN

Will you despise the king, and scorn him so?

131 *he* (Q shee) cf. reverse error at I. iii, 63
141 *live in grave* save one's soul
142 *erect* raise in dignity
145 *What though* even supposing that
147 Q assigns to Ateukin
     no power to rule ed. (Q to power no rule)
153 *move* solicit   155 *pretends* designs, intends

IDA

In all allegiance I will serve his grace,
But not in lust, oh how I blush to name it!

ATEUKIN

[*Aside*] An endless work is this, how should I frame it?

They discourse privately

SLIPPER

Oh mistress may I turn a word upon you?   160

COUNTESS

Friend what wilt thou?

SLIPPER

Oh what a happy gentlewoman be you truly, the world
reports this of you mistress, that a man can no sooner
come to your house, but the butler comes with a blackjack
and says, welcome friend, here's a cup of the best for you,   165
verily mistress you are said to have the best ale in all
Scotland.

COUNTESS

Sirrah go fetch him drink. [SERVANT *brings ale*] How likest
thou this?

SLIPPER

Like it mistress? Why, this is quincy quarie pepper de   170
watchet, single goby, of all that ever I tasted: I'll prove in
this ale and toast, the compass of the whole world. First,
this is the earth, it lies in the middle, a fair brown toast, a
goodly country for hungry teeth to dwell upon: next, this is
the sea, a fair pool for a dry tongue to fish in: now come I,   175
and seeing the world is naught, I divide it thus, and because
the sea cannot stand without the earth, as Aristotle saith, I
put them both into their first chaos, which is my belly, and
so mistress you may see your ale is become a miracle.

EUSTACE

A merry mate madam, I promise you.   180

COUNTESS

Why sigh you sirrah?

160 *turn a word upon* direct a word to (*OED turn* V 26)
161 Q assigns to Ateukin
164 *blackjack* leather jug for beer (*OED*'s earliest example is from
    1591)
170–171 *quincy . . . goby* nonce-words
173 *lies* ed. (Q ties)
177 *as Aristotle saith* in *De Caelo*, II, 13
180 *mate* fellow

SLIPPER

Truly madam, to think upon the world, which since I
denounced it, keeps such a rumbling in my stomach, that
unless your cook give it a counterbuff with some of your
roasted capons or beef, I fear me I shall become a loose   185
body, so dainty I think, I shall neither hold fast before
nor behind.

COUNTESS

Go take him in and feast this merry swain,
Sirrah, my cook is your physician,
He hath a purge for to digest the world.   190

[Exeunt SLIPPER *and* SERVANT]

ATEUKIN

Will you not, Ida, grant his highness this?

IDA

As I have said, in duty I am his:
For other lawless lusts, that ill beseem him,
I cannot like, and good I will not deem him.

COUNTESS

Ida, come in, and sir if so you please,   195
Come take a homely widow's entertain.

IDA

If he have no great haste, he may come nigh.
If haste, though he be gone, I will not cry.

Exeunt [COUNTESS, IDA, *and* EUSTACE]

ATEUKIN

I see this labour lost, my hope in vain,
Yet will I try another drift again.   200

[Exit]

[Act II, Scene ii]

Enter the BISHOP OF ST. ANDREWS, EARL DOUGLAS, MORTON,
with others, one way, the QUEEN *with* NANO *another way*

BISHOP

Oh wrack of Commonweal! Oh wretched state!

DOUGLAS

Oh hapless flock whereas the guide is blind!

183 *denounced* gave authoritative information about
186 *dainty* delicate in health
190 *digest* help the digestion of (antedates *OED*'s earliest example,
    from 1607)
s.d. NANO ed. (Q Dwarfes)
   2 *whereas* where

They all are in a muse

MORTON

Oh heedless youth, where counsel is despised.

DOROTHEA

Come pretty knave, and prank it by my side.

Let's see your best attendance out of hand.   5

NANO

Madam although my limbs are very small,

My heart is good, I'll serve you therewithal.

DOROTHEA

How if I were assailed, what couldst thou do?

NANO

Madam, call help, and boldly fight it too,

Although a bee be but a little thing,   10

You know fair queen, it hath a bitter sting.

DOROTHEA

How couldst thou do me good were I in grief?

NANO

Counsel dear princess, is a choice relief.

Though Nestor wanted force, great was his wit,

And though I am but weak, my words are fit.   15

BISHOP

[*Aside*] Like to a ship upon the ocean seas,

Tossed in the doubtful stream without a helm,

Such is a monarch without good advice.

I am o'erheard, cast rein upon thy tongue,

Andrews beware, reproof will breed a scar.   20

MORTON

Good day my lord.

BISHOP   Lord Morton well y-met:

Whereon deems Lord Douglas all this while?

DOUGLAS

Of that which yours and my poor heart doth break

Although fear shuts our mouths: we dare not speak.

DOROTHEA

[*Aside*] What mean these princes sadly to consult?   25

Somewhat I fear, betideth them amiss,

They are so pale in looks, so vexed in mind:

—In happy hour ye noble Scottish peers

Have I encountered you, what makes you mourn?

4 *prank it* strut

6 NANO (Q gives Nano's s.p. as *Dwarfe* throughout this scene)

14 *Nestor* the oldest and wisest Greek chief in the Trojan war

22 *deems* ponders   28 *ye* ed. (Q the)

BISHOP
    If we with patience may attention gain,   30
    Your grace shall know the cause of all our grief.

DOROTHEA
    Speak on good father, come and sit by me:
    I know thy care is for the common good.

BISHOP
    As fortune mighty princess reareth some,
    To high estate, and place in commonweal,   35
    So by divine bequest to them is lent,
    A riper judgement and more searching eye,
    Whereby they may discern the common harm,
    For where our fortunes in the world are most,
    Where all our profits rise and still increase,   40
    There is our mind, thereon we meditate,
    And what we do partake of good advice,
    That we employ for to conserve the same.
    To this intent these nobles and myself,
    That are (or should be) eyes of commonweal,   45
    Seeing his highness' reckless course of youth,
    His lawless and unbridled vain in love,
    His too intentive trust to flatterers,
    His abject care of counsel and his friends,
    Cannot but grieve, and since we cannot draw   50
    His eye or judgement to discern his faults,
    Since we have spake and counsel is not heard,
    I for my part, (let others as they list)
    Will leave the court, and leave him to his will:
    Lest with a ruthful eye I should behold   55
    His overthrow, which sore I fear is nigh.

DOROTHEA
    Ah father are you so estranged from love,
    From due allegiance to your prince and land,
    To leave your king when most he needs your help.
    The thrifty husbandmen are never wont,   60
    That see their lands unfruitful, to forsake them:
    But when the mould is barren and unapt,
    They toil, they plough, and make the fallow fat:

30 *attention* ed. (Q attentiue)
39 *our fortunes* ed. (Q importunes)
43 *conserve* ed. (Q concerne)
47 *vain* vanity
48 *intentive* heedful, attentive
49 *abject* rejected

The pilot in the dangerous seas is known,
In calmer waves the silly sailor strives.   65
Are you not members, lords, of commonweal,
And can your head, your dear anointed king,
Default, ye lords, except yourselves do fail?
Oh stay your steps, return and counsel him.

DOUGLAS
Men seek not moss upon a rolling stone,   70
Or water from the sieve, or fire from ice:
Or comfort from a reckless monarch's hands.
Madam, he sets us light that served in court,
In place of credit in his father's days,
If we but enter presence of his grace,   75
Our payment is a frown, a scoff, a frump,
Whilst flattering Gnato pranks it by his side,
Soothing the careless king in his misdeeds,
And if your grace consider your estate,
His life should urge you too if all be true.   80

DOROTHEA
Why, Douglas, why?

DOUGLAS   As if you have not heard
His lawless love to Ida grown of late,
His careless estimate of your estate.

DOROTHEA
Ah Douglas thou misconstrest his intent,
He doth but tempt his wife, he tries my love: 85
This injury pertains to me, not to you.
The king is young, and if he step awry,
He may amend, and I will love him still.
Should we disdain our vines because they sprout
Before their time? Or young men if they strain   90
Beyond their reach? No, vines that bloom and spread
Do promise fruits, and young men that are wild,
In age grow wise. My friends and Scottish peers,
If that an English princess may prevail,
Stay, stay with him, lo how my zealous prayer   95
Is plead with tears, fie peers, will you hence?

76 *frump* jeer
77 *Gnato* Ateukin
   pranks it struts
81 *Why . . . why?* (Q assigns to Douglas)

---

70 *moss . . . stone.* Cf. 'A rolling stone gathers no moss' (*Tilley* S 885).
71 *water . . . sieve.* Cf. 'To pour water into a sieve' (*Tilley* W 111).

BISHOP
    Madam 'tis virtue in your grace to plead,
    But we that see his vain untoward course,
    Cannot but fly the fire before it burn,
    And shun the court before we see his fall.   100
DOROTHEA
    Will you not stay? Then lordings fare you well.
    Though you forsake your king, the heavens I hope
    Will favour him through mine incessant prayer.
NANO
    Content you madam, thus old Ovid sings:
    'Tis foolish to bewail recureless things.   105
DOROTHEA
    Peace dwarf, these words my patience move.
NANO
    Although you charm my speech, charm not my love.
                   Exeunt NANO, DOROTHEA

    Enter the KING OF SCOTS, *the nobles spying him, returns*

KING OF SCOTS
    Douglas how now? Why changest thou thy cheer?
DOUGLAS
    My private troubles are so great my liege,
    As I must crave your licence for a while,   110
    For to intend mine own affairs at home.
KING OF SCOTS
    You may depart, *Exit* [DOUGLAS] but why is Morton sad?
MORTON
    The like occasion doth import me too,
    So I desire your grace to give me leave.
KING OF SCOTS
    Well sir you may betake you to your ease,   115

108 s.d. KING OF SCOTS (Q King of Scots, Arius)
111 *intend* look after
112 s.d. (Q aligns with 111)
113 *import* concern
116 *let* hindrance

104–105 *Ovid . . . things.* Cf. 'What cannot be cured must be endured'
    (*Tilley* C 922).
106 *Peace dwarf.* Dyce notes that an epithet seems to have dropped out;
    Grosart supplies *foolish*; Collins conjectures *prating*.
108 s.d. Arius occurs as the name of the King of England in the s.p.'s at
    V. iii, 1, 11, 32, 34 in Q.

When such grim sirs are gone, I see no let
To work my will.
BISHOP   What, like the eagle then,
  With often flight wilt thou thy feathers lose?
  O king canst thou endure to see thy court
  Of finest wits and judgements dispossessed,   120
  Whilst cloaking craft with soothing climbs so high,
  As each bewails ambition is so bad?
  Thy father left thee with estate and crown,
  A learned council to direct thy court,
  These carelessly O king thou castest off,   125
  To entertain a train of sycophants:
  Thou well may'st see, although thou wilt not see,
  That every eye and ear both sees and hears
  The certain signs of thine incontinence:
  Thou art allied unto the English king,   130
  By marriage: a happy friend indeed,
  If used well, if not, a mighty foe.
  Thinketh your grace he can endure and brook,
  To have a partner in his daughter's love?
  Thinketh your grace the grudge of privy wrongs   135
  Will not procure him change his smiles to threats?
  Oh be not blind to good, call home your lords,
  Displace these flattering Gnatos, drive them hence:
  Love and with kindness take your wedlock wife,
  Or else (which God forbid) I fear a change,   140
  Sin cannot thrive in courts without a plague.
KING OF SCOTS
  Go pack thou too, unless thou mend thy talk:
  On pain of death proud bishop get you gone,
  Unless you headless mean to hop away.
BISHOP
  Thou God of heaven prevent my country's fall.   145

                                                          Exit

KING OF SCOTS
  These stays and lets to pleasure plague my thoughts,
  Forcing my grievous wounds anew to bleed:
  But care that hath transported me so far,
  Fair Ida, is dispersed in thought of thee,

124 *court* all eds. but Manly emend to *course*, but Q makes sense
142 *pack* depart

117–118 *eagle . . . lose.* Not recorded in *Tilley* or W. M. Carroll, *Animal
   Conventions in English Renaissance Non-Religious Prose.*

Whose answer yields me life, or breeds my death: 150
Yond comes the messenger of weal or woe.

Enter ATEUKIN

Ateukin what news?

ATEUKIN
The adamant O king will not be filed,
But by itself, and beauty that exceeds,
By some exceeding favour must be wrought.   155
Ida is coy as yet, and doth repine,
Objecting marriage, honour, fear, and death,
She's holy, wise, and too precise for me.

KING OF SCOTS
Are these thy fruits of wits, thy sight in art?
Thine eloquence, thy policy, thy drift,   160
To mock thy prince? Then caitiff pack thee hence,
And let me die devoured in my love.

ATEUKIN
Good lord how rage gainsayeth reason's power,
My dear, my gracious, and beloved prince,
The essence of my suit, my god on earth,   165
Sit down and rest yourself, appease your wrath,
Lest with a frown ye wound me to the death:
Oh that I were included in my grave,
That either now to save my prince's life,
Must counsel cruelty, or lose my king.   170

KING OF SCOTS
Why sirrah, is there means to move her mind?

ATEUKIN
Oh should I not offend my royal liege.

KING OF SCOTS
Tell all, spare naught, so I may gain my love.

ATEUKIN
Alas my soul why art thou torn in twain,
For fear thou talk a thing that should displease?   175

KING OF SCOTS
Tut, speak whatso thou wilt, I pardon thee.

ATEUKIN
How kind a word, how courteous is his grace:

151 s.d. ATEUKIN ed. (Q Gnato)
158 *precise* scrupulous   168 *included* enclosed within

---

165 *suit*. All eds. emend to *soul* or *soule*, but Ateukin is referring to the
errand from which he has just returned, and in connection with which
he has twice used the same word (at II. i, 123 and 144).

Who would not die to succour such a king?
My liege, this lovely maid of modest mind,
Could well incline to love, but that she fears   180
Fair Dorothea's power: your grace doth know
Your wedlock is a mighty let to love:
Were Ida sure to be your wedded wife,
That then the twig would bow, you might command.
Ladies love presents, pomp, and high estate.   185

KING OF SCOTS
Ah Ateukin, how should we displace this let?

ATEUKIN
Tut mighty prince, oh that I might be whist.

KING OF SCOTS
Why dalliest thou?

ATEUKIN   I will not move my prince,
I will prefer his safety before my life:
Hear me O king, 'tis Dorothea's death   190
Must do you good.

KING OF SCOTS   What, murther of my queen?
Yet to enjoy my love, what is my queen?
Oh but my vow and promise to my queen,
Aye but my hope to gain a fairer queen:
With how contrarious thoughts am I withdrawn!   195
Why linger I 'twixt hope and doubtful fear:
If Dorothea die, will Ida love?

ATEUKIN
She will my lord.

KING OF SCOTS
Then let her die. Devise, advise the means,
All likes me well that lends me hope in love.   200

ATEUKIN
What, will your grace consent, then let me work:
There's here in court a Frenchman, Jaques called,
A fit performer of our enterprise,
Whom I by gifts and promise will corrupt,
To slay the queen, so that your grace will seal   205
A warrant for the man to save his life.

KING OF SCOTS
Naught shall he want, write thou and I will sign,
And gentle Gnato, if my Ida yield,

186 *displace* ed. (Q *display*)
187 *whist* silent
199 *Then . . . means,* (Q . . . die./Deuise . . .)
205 *so that* provided that

Thou shalt have what thou wilt, I'll give thee straight,
A barony, an earldom for reward.   210

ATEUKIN
Frolic young king, the lass shall be your own,
I'll make her blithe and wanton by my wit.   *Exeunt*

Chorus

Enter BOHAN *with* OBERON

BOHAN
So Oberon, now it begins to work in kind,
The ancient lords by leaving him alone,
Disliking of his humours and despite,
Lets him run headlong, till his flatterers,
Sweetening his thoughts of luckless lust,   5
With vile persuasions and alluring words,
Makes him make way by murther to his will.
Judge fairy king, hast heard a greater ill?

OBERON
Nor seen more virtue in a country maid.
I tell thee Bohan it doth make me sorry,   10
To think the deeds the king means to perform.

BOHAN
To change that humour stand and see the rest,
I trow my son Slipper will show's a jest.

Enter SLIPPER *with a companion, boy or wench, dancing a hornpipe, and dance out again*

BOHAN
Now after this beguiling of our thoughts,
And changing them from sad to better glee,   15
Let's to our cell, and sit and see the rest,
For I believe this jig will prove no jest.   *Exeunt*

211 *Frolic* be merry
2 *alone* ed. (Q aliue)   3 *despite* ed. (Q respight)
5 *Sweetening* ed. (Q Sweeting)   9 *seen* ed. (Q send)
10 *sorry* ed. (Q merrie)   15 *glee* mirth

1 Heading *Chorus*. This word is obviously misplaced in Q after line 17, as part of the heading to Act III, since it is the Bohan–Oberon scenes which are referred to as the Chorus.

17 *jig*. Drama, play (not recorded by *OED*); perhaps an extension of *OED* 5 'a trifle' (earliest example 1592). But clearly here and elsewhere (see note to V. Chorus, 12) Bohan uses the word to refer to the play of which he is the presenter.

[Act III, Scene i]

Actus Tertius . . . Scena Prima

Enter SLIPPER *one way, and* SIR BARTRAM *another way*

SIR BARTRAM
Ho fellow, stay and let me speak with thee.
SLIPPER
Fellow? Friend thou dost disbuse me, I am a gentleman.
SIR BARTRAM
A gentleman, how so?
SLIPPER
Why, I rub horses sir.
SIR BARTRAM
And what of that?   5
SLIPPER
Oh simple witted, mark my reason: they that do good
service in the commonweal are gentlemen, but such as rub
horses do good service in the commonweal, ergo, tarbox
master courtier, a horse-keeper is a gentleman.
SIR BARTRAM
[*Aside*] Here is over-much wit in good earnest:—but sirrah   10
where is thy master?
SLIPPER
Neither above ground nor under ground, drawing out red
into white, swallowing that down without chawing, that
was never made without treading.
SIR BARTRAM
Why where is he then?   15
SLIPPER
Why, in his cellar, drinking a cup of neat and brisk claret,
in a bowl of silver: Oh sir, the wine runs trillill down his
throat, which cost the poor vintner many a stamp before it
was made: but I must hence sir, I have haste.
SIR BARTRAM
Why, whither now I prithee?   20
SLIPPER
Faith sir, to Sir Silvester, a knight hard by, upon my

2 *disbuse* malapropism for *abuse*
8 *tarbox* stinking fellow (earliest example in *OED*)
10–15 Q prints as verse (. . . earnest:/But . . .)
17 *trillill* with the sound of flowing liquid (earliest example in
    OED)

master's errand, whom I must certify this, that the lease of
East Spring shall be confirmed, and therefore must I bid
him provide trash, for my master is no friend without
money.   25

SIR BARTRAM
    [*Aside*] This is the thing for which I sued so long,
    This is the lease which I by Gnato's means,
    Sought to possess by patent from the king:
    But he injurious man, who lives by crafts,
    And sells king's favours for who will give most,   30
    Hath taken bribes of me, yet covertly
    Will sell away the thing pertains to me:
    But I have found a present help I hope,
    For to prevent his purpose and deceit:
    —Stay gentle friend.   35

SLIPPER
    A good word, thou hast won me. This word is like a warm
    caudle to a cold stomach.

SIR BARTRAM
    Sirrah wilt thou for money and reward convey me certain
    letters out of hand, from out thy master's pocket?

SLIPPER
    Will I sir, why, were it to rob my father, hang my mother, or   40
    any such like trifles, I am at your commandment sir, what
    will you give me sir?

SIR BARTRAM
    A hundred pounds.

SLIPPER
    I am your man, give me earnest, I am dead at a pocket sir,
    why I am a lifter, master, by my occupation.   45

24 *trash* money (earliest example in *OED*)
36–37 Q prints as verse (. . . me,/This . . .)
37 *caudle* ed. (Q candle)
38–39 Q prints as verse (. . . reward,/Conuay . . . hand,/From . . .)
38 *convey* steal
44 *earnest* sum of money sealing the contract, part of the total
    amount
    dead unerring, sure (earliest example in *OED*)
45 *lifter* thief (earliest example in *OED*)

_____

37 *caudle*. The same mistake occurs in the Folio and Q2 texts of *Love's
    Labour's Lost*, IV. iii, 172, and the Folio text of *2 Henry VI*, IV. vii. 95,
    the only two uses by Shakespeare of the word as a noun. A warm thin
    drink of gruel and ale, or wine, with sugar, given to women, children,
    and especially invalids.

SIR BARTRAM

A lifter, what is that?

SLIPPER

Why sir, I can lift a pot as well as any man, and pick a purse
as soon as any thief in my country.

SIR BARTRAM

Why fellow, hold, here is earnest, ten pound to assure
thee, go dispatch, and bring it me to yonder tavern thou   50
seest, and assure thyself thou shalt both have thy skin full
of wine, and the rest of thy money.

SLIPPER

I will sir. Now room for a gentleman, my masters, who
gives me money for a fair new angel, a trim new angel?

Exeunt

[Act III, Scene ii]

Enter ANDREW *and* PURVEYOR

PURVEYOR

Sirrah, I must needs have your master's horses, the king
cannot be unserved.

ANDREW

Sirrah you must needs go without them, because my master
must be served.

PURVEYOR

Why, I am the king's purveyor, and I tell thee I will have   5
them.

ANDREW

I am Ateukin's servant, Signior Andrew, and I say thou
shalt not have them.

PURVEYOR

Here's my ticket, deny it if thou dar'st.

ANDREW

There is the stable, fetch them out if thou dar'st.   10

49-52 Q prints as verse (earnest,/Ten . . . dispatch,/And . . . seest,/
   And . . . haue/Thy . . .)
54 *money* change (not recorded in *OED*)
   angel gold coin worth ten shillings
1-8 Q prints as verse (. . . horses,/The . . . ; . . . them,/Because
   . . . ; . . . Purueyer,/And . . . ; . . . Andrew,/And . . .)
5 *the king's purveyor* official who requisitioned horses, vehicles, and
   provisions for the sovereign
9 *ticket* licence, warrant

PURVEYOR

Sirrah, sirrah, tame your tongue, lest I make you.

ANDREW

Sirrah, sirrah, hold your hand, lest I bum you.

PURVEYOR

I tell thee, thy master's geldings are good, and therefore fit for the king.

ANDREW

I tell thee, my master's horses have galled backs, and there-   15
fore cannot fit the king. Purveyor, purveyor, purvey thee
of more wit: dar'st thou presume to wrong my Lord
Ateukin, being the chiefest man in court?

PURVEYOR

[*Aside*] The more unhappy commonweal, where flatterers
are chief in court.   20

ANDREW

What sayest thou?

PURVEYOR

I say thou art too presumptuous, and the officers shall
school thee.

ANDREW

A fig for them and thee purveyor, they seek a knot in a ring,
that would wrong my master or his servants in this court.   25

Enter JAQUES

PURVEYOR

The world is at a wise pass, when nobility is afraid of a
flatterer.

JAQUES

Sirrah, what be you that parley *contre Monsieur* my Lord
Ateukin, *en bonne foi*, prate you against Sir *Altesse*, me
maka your *tête* to leap from your shoulders, *par ma foi c'y*   30
ferai-je.

12 *bum* beat, thump
13–16 Q prints as verse (. . . good,/And . . . ; . . . backes,/And . . .)
19–20 Q prints as verse (. . . Common-weale,/Where . . .)
22–27 Q prints as verse (. . . presumptuous,/And . . . ; . . .
Purueyer,/They . . . wrong/My . . . ; . . . passe,/When . . .)
24 *a fig for* expression of contempt, perhaps with indecent sense
seek a knot in a ring make difficulties where there are none
28 *parley contre* speak against
29 *en bonne foi* on my word
30 *Altesse* Highness
tête head
30–31 *par . . . ferai-je* on my word I will do it

ANDREW

Oh signior captain, you show yourself a forward and
friendly gentleman in my master's behalf, I will cause him
to thank you.

JAQUES

Poltron, speak me one *parola* against my *bon gentilhomme*,   35
I shall *estamp* your guts, and thump your backa, that you *ne*
point manage this ten hours.

PURVEYOR

Sirrah come open me the stable, and let me have the horses:
and fellow, for all your French brags I will do my duty.

ANDREW

I'll make garters of thy guts thou villain, if thou enter this   40
office.

JAQUES

Mort Dieu, take me that cappa *pour votre labeur*, be gone
vilain, in the *mort*.

PURVEYOR

What, will you resist me then? Well the council, fellow,
shall know of your insolency.   *Exit*   45

ANDREW

Tell them what thou wilt, and eat that I can best spare
from my back parts, and get you gone with a vengeance.

Enter ATEUKIN

ATEUKIN

Andrew.

ANDREW

Sir.

35 *Poltron* milksop
    parola word (Italian)
    bon gentilhomme fine gentleman
36 *estamp* ed. (Q estrampe) stamp
    ne ed. (Q no)
37–38 *ne point* will not
37 *hours* ed. (Q ours)
38–45 Q prints as verse (. . . stable,/And . . . horses:/And . . . ;
    . . . guttes,/Thou . . . ; . . . cappa/Pour . . . ; . . . then?/Well
    . . .)
41 *office* outbuilding, stable
42 *Mortdieu* ed. (Q Mort lieu) zounds
    votre ed. (Q nostre)
    cappa trifle (Italian)
    pour votre labeur for your trouble
43 *in the mort* to hell (?)   47 s.d. ATEUKIN ed. (Q Gnato)

ATEUKIN

Where be my writings I put in my pocket last night?   50

ANDREW

Which, sir, your annotations upon Machiavel?

ATEUKIN

No sir, the letters patents for East Spring.

ANDREW

Why sir you talk wonders to me, if you ask that question.

ATEUKIN

Yea sir, and will work wonders too with you, unless you
find them out, villain search me them out and bring them   55
me, or thou art but dead.

ANDREW

A terrible word in the latter end of a sessions. Master
were you in your right wits yesternight?

ATEUKIN

Dost thou doubt it?

ANDREW

Aye and why not sir, for the greatest clerks are not the   60
wisest, and a fool may dance in a hood, as well as a wise
man in a bare frock: besides, such as give themselves to
philautia, as you do master, are so choleric of complexion,
that that which they burn in fire over night, they seek for
with fury the next morning. Ah, I take care of your worship,   65
this commonweal should have a great loss of so good a
member as you are.

ATEUKIN

Thou flatterest me.

ANDREW

Is it flattery in me sir to speak you fair? What is it then in
you to dally with the king?   70

ATEUKIN

Are you prating knave? I will teach you better nurture! Is

54 *with* ed. (Q which)
63 *philautia* ed. (Q Plulantia) self-love, conceit
69–73 Q prints as verse (. . . faire?/What . . . ; . . . knaue,/I . . .
        nurture?/Is . . . wardrop?/Of . . .)
71 *nurture* breeding, manners

56–57 *thou . . . sessions.* Apparently a reference to the death-sentence,
     though the phrase 'thou art but dead' seems not to have been part of the
     sentencing formula (*but* = absolutely; *OED* B 6 b).
60–61 *greatest . . . wisest.* Cf. *Tilley* C 409.
61 *a fool . . . hood.* Cf. *Tilley* H 586.

this the care you have of my wardrobe? Of my accounts,
and matters of trust?

ANDREW

Why alas sir, in times past your garments have been so
well inhabited, as your tenants would give no place to a　75
moth to mangle them, but since you are grown greater and
your garments more fine and gay, if your garments are not
fit for hospitality, blame your pride, and commend my
cleanliness: as for your writings, I am not for them, nor
they for me.　　80

ATEUKIN

Villain go, fly, find them out: if thou losest them, thou
losest my credit.

ANDREW

Alas sir, can I lose that you never had?

ATEUKIN

Say you so, then hold, feel you that you never felt.

[Beats him]

JAQUES

Oh *monsieur, ayez patience*, pardon your *pauvre valet*,　85
me be at your commandment.

ATEUKIN

Signior Jaques, well met, you shall command me, sirrah go
cause my writings be proclaimed in the market-place,
promise a great reward to them that finds them, look where
I supped and everywhere.　　90

ANDREW

I will sir: *[Aside]* now are two knaves well met, and three well
parted, if you conceive mine enigma gentlemen. What
shall I be then, faith, a plain harp shilling.　　*Exit*

ATEUKIN

Sieur Jaques, this our happy meeting rids
Your friends and me, of care and grievous toil,　　95

81–82 Q prints as verse (. . . out:/If . . .)
85–86 Q prints as verse (. . . vallet,/Me . . .)
85 *monsieur, ayez patience* sir, have patience
　　pauvre valet poor manservant
87–90 Q prints as verse　(. . . me,/Sirra . . . place,/Promise . . .
　　them,/Looke . . .)
92 *conceive* understand
94 *rids* ed. (Q hides)

93 *a plain harp shilling*. A brass coin value one penny, current in Ireland in
　　the late sixteenth century (= worth very little?).

For I that look into deserts of men,
And see among the soldiers in this court
A noble forward mind, and judge thereof,
Cannot but seek the means to raise them up
Who merit credit in the commonweal.   100
To this intent friend Jaques I have found
A means to make you great, and well esteemed,
Both with the king, and with the best in court:
For I espy in you a valiant mind,
Which makes me love, admire, and honour you: 105
To this intent (if so your trust and faith,
Your secrecy, be equal with your force)
I will impart a service to thyself,
Which if thou dost effect, the king, myself,
And what or he, and I with him can work,   110
Shall be employed in what thou wilt desire.

JAQUES
Me sweara by my ten bones, my *signior*, to be loyal to your
lordship's intents, affairs, yea my *monseigneur*, *que non
ferai-je pour* your pleasure? By my sworda me be no *babillard*.

ATEUKIN
Then hoping on thy truth, I prithee see   115
How kind Ateukin is to forward thee,
Hold, take this earnest penny of my love,

[*Gives money*]

And mark my words, the king by me requires
No slender service Jaqu̇es, at thy hands.
Thou must by privy practice make away   120
The queen, fair Dorothea, as she sleeps:
Or how thou wilt, so she be done to death:
Thou shalt not want promotion here in court.

JAQUES
Stabba the woman, *par ma foi, monseigneur*, me thrusta

113 *yea* ed. (Q ye)
113–114 *my monseigneur . . . ferai-je* my lord, what would I not do for
114 *your* ed. (Q Yea)
     By . . . babillard (Q prints as a verse line)
     babillard ed. (Q babie Lords) chatterbox
116 *thee* ed. (Q mee)
117 *earnest penny* partial payment sealing the contract
124 *par . . . monseigneur* on my word, sir

112 *my signior* ed. (Q my singniar). Other eds. read *monseigneur*, but Jaques is
an Italianate Frenchman.

my weapon into her belly, so me may be guard *par le roi*.   125
Me do your service. But me no be hanged *pour* my labour.

ATEUKIN

Thou shalt have warrant Jaques from the king,
None shall outface, gainsay and wrong my friend.
Do not I love thee Jaques? Fear not then,
I tell thee whoso toucheth thee in aught,   130
Shall injure me, I love, I tender thee:
Thou art a subject fit to serve his grace.
Jaques, I had a written warrant once,
But that by great misfortune late is lost,
Come wend we to St. Andrews, where his grace   135
Is now in progress, where he shall assure
Thy safety, and confirm thee to the act.

JAQUES

We will attend your nobleness.   *Exeunt*

[Act III, Scene iii]

Enter SIR BARTRAM, DOROTHEA *the* queen, NANO, LORD ROSS,
Ladies attendants

DOROTHEA

Thy credit Bartram in the Scottish court,
Thy reverend years, the strictness of thy vows,
All these are means sufficient to persuade,
But love the faithful link of loyal hearts,
That hath possession of my constant mind,   5
Exiles all dread, subdueth vain suspect,
Methinks no craft should harbour in that breast,
Where majesty and virtue is installed:
Methinks my beauty should not cause my death.

SIR BARTRAM

How gladly sovereign princess would I err,   10
And blind my shame to save your royal life:
'Tis princely in yourself to think the best,
To hope his grace is guiltless of this crime,
But if in due prevention you default,
How blind are you that were forewarned before.   15

125 *par le roi* by the king
126 Q prints as verse (. . . seruice./But . . .)
      pour for
136 *in progress* on a state visit
  9 *Methinks* ed. (Q Me thinke)   11 *blind* ed. (Q binde)

DOROTHEA
Suspicion without cause deserveth blame.
SIR BARTRAM
Who see, and shun not harms, deserve the same:
Behold the tenor of this traitorous plot.

[*Shows warrant*]

DOROTHEA
What should I read? Perhaps he wrote it not.
SIR BARTRAM
Here is his warrant under seal and sign,   20
To Jaques born in France, to murther you.
DOROTHEA
Ah careless king, would God this were not thine.
What though I read? Ah, should I think it true?
ROSS
The hand and seal confirms the deed is his.
DOROTHEA
What know I though, if now he thinketh this?   25
NANO
Madam, Lucretius saith, that to repent,
Is childish, wisdom to prevent.
DOROTHEA   What though?
NANO
Then cease your tears, that have dismayed you,
And cross the foe before he have betrayed you.
SIR BARTRAM
What needs these long suggestions in this cause,   30
When every circumstance confirmeth truth?
First let the hidden mercy from above
Confirm your grace, since by a wondrous means
The practice of your dangers came to light:
Next let the tokens of approved truth   35
Govern and stay your thoughts, too much seduced,
And mark the sooth, and listen the intent.
Your highness knows, and these my noble lords
Can witness this, that whilst your husband's sire
In happy peace possessed the Scottish crown,   40

24 *hand* handwriting   30 *this* ed. (Q there)

---

26 *Lucretius saith*. Collins: 'there is no such sentiment in Lucretius.'; but see
De Rerum Natura, iv. 1144–1145: 'ut melius vigilare sit ante,/qua docuit
ratione, cavereque ne inliciaris'—'so that it is better to be on guard before-
hand as I have explained, and to take care that you are not enticed'. See
also *Tilley* P 569: 'Prevention is better than cure' (earliest example 1618).

I was his sworn attendant here in court,
In dangerous fight I never failed my lord.
And since his death, and this your husband's reign,
No labour, duty, have I left undone,
To testify my zeal unto the crown: 45
But now my limbs are weak, mine eyes are dim,
Mine age unwieldy and unmeet for toil:
I came to court, in hope for service past,
To gain some lease to keep me, being old.
There found I all was upsy-turvy turned,   50
My friends displaced, the nobles loth to crave,
Then sought I to the minion of the king,
Ateukin, who allured by a bribe,
Assured me of the lease for which I sought:
But see the craft, when he had got the grant,   55
He wrought to sell it to Sir Silvester,
In hope of greater earnings from his hands:
In brief, I learnt his craft, and wrought the means,
By one his needy servant, for reward
To steal from out his pocket all the briefs,   60
Which he performed, and with reward resigned.
Them when I read (now mark the power of God)
I found this warrant sealed among the rest,
To kill your grace, whom God long keep alive.
Thus in effect, by wonder are you saved,   65
Trifle not then, but seek a speedy flight,
God will conduct your steps, and shield the right.
DOROTHEA
What should I do, ah poor unhappy queen?
Born to endure what fortune can contain,
Alas the deed is too apparent now: 70
But oh mine eyes, were you as bent to hide,
As my poor heart is forward to forgive,
Ah cruel king, my love would thee acquit.
Oh what avails to be allied and matched
With high estates that marry but in show?   75
Were I baser born, my mean estate
Could warrant me from this impendent harm,
But to be great and happy, these are twain.
Ah Ross what shall I do, how shall I work?

51 *crave* ask for favours   59 *servant* ed. (Q seruants)
66 *speedy* ed. (Q speakie)
78 *twain* separate, opposed (*OED*'s earliest example is from
   Shakespeare's sonnets [1600])

ROSS

    With speedy letters to your father send,   80
    Who will revenge you, and defend your right.

DOROTHEA

    As if they kill not me, who with him fight!
    As if his breast be touched, I am not wounded,
    As if he wailed, my joys were not confounded:
    We are one heart, though rent by hate in twain: 85
    One soul, one essence doth our weal contain:
    What then can conquer him that kills not me?

ROSS

    If this advice displease, then madam flee.

DOROTHEA

    Where may I wend or travel without fear?

NANO

    Where not, in changing this attire you wear?   90

DOROTHEA

    What, shall I clad me like a country maid?

NANO

    The policy is base I am afraid.

DOROTHEA

    Why Nano?

NANO   Ask you why? What, may a queen
    March forth in homely weed and be not seen?
    The rose although in thorny shrubs she spread,   95
    Is still the rose, her beauties wax not dead.
    And noble minds although the coat be bare,
    Are by their semblance known, how great they are.

SIR BARTRAM

    The dwarf saith true.

DOROTHEA   What garments lik'st thou then?

NANO

    Such as may make you seem a proper man.   100

DOROTHEA

    He makes me blush and smile, though I am sad.

NANO

    The meanest coat for safety is not bad.

DOROTHEA

    What, shall I jet in breeches like a squire?
    Alas poor dwarf, thy mistress is unmeet.

103 *jet* swagger

---

104 *unmeet.* The break in rhyme suggests two lines may be missing.

NANO

    Tut, go me thus, your cloak before your face,   105
    Your sword upreared with quaint and comely grace,
    If any come and question what you be,
    Say you a man, and call for witness me.

DOROTHEA

    What, should I wear a sword, to what intent?

NANO

    Madam for show, it is an ornament,   110
    If any wrong you, draw, a shining blade
    Withdraws a coward thief that would invade.

DOROTHEA

    But if I strike, and he should strike again,
    What should I do? I fear I should be slain.

NANO

    No, take it single on your dagger so,   115
    I'll teach you madam how to ward a blow.

DOROTHEA

    How little shapes much substance may include!
    Sir Bartram, Ross, ye ladies and my friends,
    Since presence yields me death, and absence life,
    Hence will I fly disguised like a squire,   120
    As one that seeks to live in Irish wars,
    You gentle Ross, shall furnish my depart.

ROSS

    Yea prince, and die with you with all my heart,
    Vouchsafe me then in all extremest states,
    To wait on you and serve you with my best.   125

DOROTHEA

    To me pertains the woe, live then in rest:
    Friends, fare you well, keep secret my depart,
    Nano alone shall my attendant be.

NANO

    Then madam are you manned, I warrant ye,
    Give me a sword, and if there grow debate,   130
    I'll come behind, and break your enemy's pate.

112 *Withdraws* causes to retreat
129 *manned* provided with an escort; perhaps also punning on the
    secondary meaning 'to be made a man'

---

121 *As . . . wars.* Throughout her long reign Elizabeth laboured to bring
    Ireland into complete subjection. The Irish wars were notorious for
    rape, pillage, and general savagery. For a description of them to the
    death of Greene see Cyril Falls, *Elizabeth's Irish Wars* (1950), pp. 17–173.

ROSS
  How sore we grieve to part so soon away.
DOROTHEA
  Grieve not for those that perish if they stay.
NANO
  The time in words misspent, is little worth,
  Madam walk on, and let them bring us forth.   *Exeunt*   135

Chorus

Enter BOHAN

BOHAN
  So these sad motions makes the fairy sleep,
  And sleep he shall in quiet and content,
  For it would make a marble melt and weep
  To see these treasons 'gainst the innocent:
  But since she 'scapes by flight to save her life,   5
  The king may chance repent she was his wife:
  The rest is ruthful, yet to beguile the time,
  'Tis interlaced with merriment and rhyme.   *Exit*

[Act IV, Scene i]

Actus Quartus . . . Scena Prima

After a noise of horns and shoutings, enter certain HUNTSMEN,
if you please singing, one way: another way ATEUKIN *and* JAQUES

ATEUKIN
  Say gentlemen, where may we find the king?
HUNTSMAN
  Even here at hand on hunting.
  And at this hour he taken hath a stand,
  To kill a deer.
ATEUKIN   A pleasant work in hand,
  Follow your sport, and we will seek his grace.   5
HUNTSMAN
  [*Aside*] When such him seek, it is a woeful case.
          Exeunt HUNTSMEN *one way*, ATEUKIN *and* JAQUES *another*

  1 *fairy* ed. (Q faire)
  7 *beguile* ed. (Q beguilde)
s.d. ATEUKIN *and* JAQUES ed. (Q Ateukin and Iaques, Gnato)

[Act IV, Scene ii]

Enter EUSTACE, IDA, *and the* COUNTESS

COUNTESS
    Lord Eustace, as your youth and virtuous life
    Deserves a far more fair and richer wife,
    So since I am a mother, and do wit
    What wedlock is, and that which longs to it,
    Before I mean my daughter to bestow,   5
    'Twere meet that she and I your state did know.
EUSTACE
    Madam if I consider Ida's worth,
    I know my portions merit none so fair,
    And yet I hold in farm and yearly rent,
    A thousand pound, which may her state content.   10
COUNTESS
    But what estate my lord shall she possess?
EUSTACE
    All that is mine, grave countess, and no less.
    But Ida will you love?
IDA   I cannot hate.
EUSTACE
    But will you wed?
IDA   'Tis Greek to me my lord,
    I'll wish you well, and thereon take my word.   15
EUSTACE
    Shall I some sign of favour then receive?
IDA
    Aye, if her ladyship will give me leave.
COUNTESS
    Do what thou wilt.
IDA   Then noble English peer,
    Accept this ring, wherein my heart is set,
    A constant heart, with burning flames befret: 20
    But under written this: *O morte dura*:
    Hereon when so you look with eyes *pura*,
    The maid you fancy most will favour you.

  2 *far* ed. (Q faire)
  4 *longs* belongs (*OED v*² therefore no apostrophe is needed)
  8 *portions* inheritance, possessions
20 *befret* fretted, eaten away
21 *O morte dura* O cruel death

EUSTACE
    I'll try this heart, in hope to find it true.

       Enter certain HUNTSMEN *and* LADIES

HUNTSMAN
    Widow countess well y-met,   25
    Ever may thy joys be many,
    Gentle Ida fair beset,
    Fair and wise, not fairer any:
    Frolic huntsmen of the game,
    Wills you well, and gives you greeting.   30
IDA
    Thanks good woodman for the same,
    And our sport and merry meeting.
HUNTSMAN
    Unto thee we do present,
    Silver hart with arrow wounded.
EUSTACE
    This doth shadow my lament,   35
    [With] both fear and love confounded.
LADIES
    To the mother of the maid,
    Fair as th' lilies, red as roses,
    Even so many goods are said,
    As herself in heart supposes.   40
COUNTESS
    What are you friends, that thus doth wish us well?
HUNTSMAN
    Your neighbours nigh, that have on hunting been,
    Who understanding of your walking forth,
    Prepared this train to entertain you with,
    This Lady Douglas, this Sir Egmond is.   45
COUNTESS
    Welcome ye ladies, and thousand thanks for this,
    Come enter you a homely widow's house,
    And if mine entertainment please you let us feast.
HUNTSMAN
    A lovely lady never wants a guest.
               Exeunt. Manet EUSTACE, IDA
EUSTACE
    Stay gentle Ida, tell me what you deem,   50
    What, doth this haste, this tender heart beseem?

27 *fair beset* well-bestowed (in marriage)
29 *Frolic* merry

IDA

Why not my lord, since nature teacheth art
To senseless beasts to cure their grievous smart.
Dictamnum serves to close the wound again.

EUSTACE

What help for those that love?

IDA   Why, love again.   55

EUSTACE

Were I the hart,

IDA   Then I the herb would be.
You shall not die for help, come follow me.   *Exeunt*

[Act IV, Scene iii]

Enter ANDREW *and* JAQUES

JAQUES

Mon Dieu, what *malheur* be this, me come a the chamber,
signior Andrew, *mon Dieu*, taka my *poignard en mon main*, to
give the *estocade* to the *damoisella*, *par ma foi*, there was no
person, *elle s'est en allée.*

ANDREW

The worse luck Jaques, but because I am thy friend I will   5
advise thee somewhat towards the attainment of the gallows.

JAQUES

Gallows, what be that?

---

  51 *haste* ed. (Q hast)
   1 *Mon Dieu* good heavens
      malheur misfortune
   2 *poignard . . . main* poniard (dagger) in my hand
   3 *estocade* stab-wound
      damoisella damsel (Italian form)
      par ma foi on my word
   4 *elle . . . allée* she was gone

---

  51 *haste.* The point of Eustace's question seems to be 'What do you think
      Ida, have we acted too hastily for your ladylike and gentle disposition?'
      (See IV. ii, 14–24 above.) She replies 'Not at all, those who are wounded
      must seek immediate relief; even senseless beasts know that.'
  52–54 A missing line should follow 53, and would be something like 'The
      struck deer feeds to ease her of her pain'.
  54 The wounded deer curing itself with Dictamnum was a common
      motif of the emblem writers, used to signify incurable love; see Henry
      Green, *Shakespeare and the Emblem Writers*, pp. 397–399.
  54 *Dictamnum* ed. (Q Dictanum). A Cretan herb supposed to have power to
      expel weapons.

ANDREW

Marry sir, a place of great promotion, where thou shalt by
one turn above ground, rid the world of a knave, and make
a goodly ensample for all bloody villains of thy profession.   10

JAQUES

Que dites-vous, monsieur Andrew?

ANDREW

I say Jaques, thou must keep this path, and hie thee, for
the queen as I am certified, is departed with her dwarf,
apparelled like a squire, overtake her Frenchman, stab her,
I'll promise thee this doublet shall be happy.   15

JAQUES

Pourquoi?

ANDREW

It shall serve a jolly gentleman, Sir Dominus Monsignior
Hangman.

JAQUES

C'est tout un, me will rama *pour la monnaie.*   [*Exit*]

ANDREW

Go, and the rot consume thee! Oh what a trim world is this!   20
My master lives by cozening the king, I by flattering him:
Slipper my fellow by stealing, and I by lying: is not this a
wily accord, gentlemen? This last night our jolly horse-
keeper being well steeped in liquor, confessed to me the
stealing of my master's writings, and his great reward: now   25
dare I not bewray him, lest he discover my knavery, but thus
have I wrought: I understand he will pass this way, to
provide him necessaries, but if I and my fellows fail not, we
will teach him such a lesson, as shall cost him a chief place
on penniless bench for his labour: but yond he comes.   30

10 *ensample* practical warning   11 JAQUES Q lacks s.p.
Que . . . Andrew? What do you say, Mr. Andrew?
15–16 *promise . . . Pourquoi* one line in Q
16 *Pourquoi?* Why?
19 *c'est tout un* it's all one   *rama* ??
pour la monnaie ed. (Q *pour le monnoie*) for the money
23 *wily accord* artful agreement
23–24 *our . . . horsekeeper* Slipper
29–30 *as . . . penniless bench* as shall reduce him to penury
31–32 one line in Q

30 *penniless bench.* Penniless bench was 'a covered bench which formerly
stood beside Carfax Church, Oxford'; the name was used 'apparently
of similar open-air seats elsewhere; probably as being the resort of
destitute wayfarers' (*OED*).

Enter SLIPPER *with a* TAILOR, *a* SHOEMAKER, *and a* CUTLER

SLIPPER
Tailor.

TAILOR
Sir.

SLIPPER
Let my doublet be white northern, five groats the yard, I
tell thee I will be brave.

TAILOR
It shall sir.   35

SLIPPER
Now sir, cut it me like the battlements of a custard, full of
round holes: edge me the sleeves with Coventry-blue, and
let the linings be of tenpenny lockram.

TAILOR
Very good sir.

SLIPPER
Make it the amorous cut, a flap before.   40

TAILOR
And why so? That fashion is stale.

SLIPPER
Oh friend, thou art a simple fellow, I tell thee a flap is a
great friend to a storrie, it stands him in stead of clean
napery, and if a man's shirt be torn, it is a present penthouse
to defend him from a clean housewife's scoff.   45

TAILOR
You say sooth sir.

SLIPPER
Hold, take thy money, there is seven shillings for the
doublet, and eight for the breeches, seven and eight,
by'rlady thirty-six is a fair deal of money.

TAILOR
Farewell sir.   50

SLIPPER
Nay but stay tailor.

33 *northern* northern cloth (*OED* records as unique example)
   groats fourpenny pieces
34 *brave* finely-dressed
43 *a storrie* qy. a stoic ?

37 *Coventry-blue*. Thread of a vivid blue chiefly used for embroidery;
   manufactured at Coventry.
38 *Lockram*. A coarse loosely-woven linen with relatively finer varieties,
   used for kerchiefs and household linen as well as linings.

TAILOR

Why sir?

SLIPPER

Forget not this special make, let my back parts be well
lined, for there come many winter storms from a windy
belly, I tell thee.   [*Exit* TAILOR]   55
Shoemaker.

SHOEMAKER

Gentleman, what shoe will it please you to have?

SLIPPER

A fine neat calves' leather my friend.

SHOEMAKER

Oh sir, that is too thin, it will not last you.

SLIPPER

I tell thee, it is my near kinsman, for I am Slipper, which   60
hath his best grace in summer to be suited in lambs' skins,
Goodwife Calf was my grandmother, and Goodman
Netherleather mine uncle, but my mother good woman,
alas, she was a Spaniard, and being well tanned and dressed
by a good fellow, an Englishman, is grown to some wealth: 65
as when I have but my upper parts clad in her husband's
costly Spanish leather, I may be bold to kiss the fairest
lady's foot in this country.

SHOEMAKER

You are of high birth sir, but have you all your mother's
marks on you?   70

SLIPPER

Why, knave?

SHOEMAKER

Because if thou come of the blood of the Slippers, you
should have a shoemaker's awl thrust through your ear.

SLIPPER

Take your earnest, friend, and be packing, and meddle not
with my progenitors.   *Exit* [SHOEMAKER]   75
Cutler.

53–56 Q prints as verse (. . . mate,/Let . . . linde,/For . . . bellie,/
    I . . .)
53 *make* ed. (Q mate) manner of construction
61 *lambs'* ed. (Q lakus)
62 *Calf* ed. (Q Clarke)
65 *good fellow* jovial person
69–70 Q prints as verse (. . . sir,/But . . .)
74–75 Q prints as verse (. . . packing,/And . . .)
74 *earnest* partial payment sealing the contract

CUTLER

Here sir.

SLIPPER

I must have a rapier and dagger.

CUTLER

A rapier and dagger you mean sir?

SLIPPER

Thou sayest true, but it must have a very fair edge.   80

CUTLER

Why so sir?

SLIPPER

Because it may cut by himself, for truly my friend, I am a
man of peace, and wear weapons but for fashion.

CUTLER

Well sir, give me earnest, I will fit you.

SLIPPER

Hold, take it, I betrust thee friend, let me be well armed.   85

CUTLER

You shall.   *Exit* CUTLER

SLIPPER

Now what remains? There's twenty crowns for a house, three
crowns for household stuff, sixpence to buy a constable's
staff: nay, I will be the chief of my parish, there wants
nothing but a wench, a cat, a dog, a wife and a servant, to   90
make an whole family, shall I marry with Alice, Goodman
Grimshaw's daughter, she is fair, but indeed her tongue is
like clocks on Shrove Tuesday, always out of temper? Shall

80 *fair* blunt (not recorded in *OED*)
88–89 *a constable's staff* sign of authority borne by parish officers

---

78 *rapier and dagger.* Apparently Slipper mispronounces the words;
   Collier suggested *reaper and digger*; *rape 'er and dig 'er* seems as likely.
92–93 *her tongue . . . Shrove Tuesday.* Shrove Tuesday, the day immediately preceding the first day of Lent, was originally the day on
   which confession was made in preparation for the penitential season,
   but in Elizabethan times was celebrated as a holiday, particularly by the
   apprentices, who indulged in mischief of various kinds, including
   tampering with clocks. For the connection of tongues and clocks, see
   Heywood's *The First Hundred of Epigrammes*, sig. O iv:
       Thy tong should be a clocke wife, had I gods power,
       For than would it strike but once in one hower,
       Yet it might ren (quoth she) and strike er the time,
       And should that clocke haue (as my tong hath) a chime?
       I beyng sexten, might set the clocke foorth soone,
       To strike and chime .xii. twoo houres before noone.

I wed Cicely of the Whighton? Oh no, she is like a frog in a
parsley bed, as skittish as an eel, if I seek to hamper her,   95
she will horn me: but a wench must be had master Slipper.
Yea and shall be dear friend.

ANDREW
I now will drive him from his contemplations. Oh my mates
come forward, the lamb is unpent, the fox shall prevail.

Enter three antics, who dance round, and take SLIPPER *with them*

SLIPPER
I will, my friend, and I thank you heartily, pray keep your   100
curtsy, I am yours in the way of an hornpipe, they are
strangers, I see they understand not my language, *oui, oui.*

Whilst they are dancing, ANDREW *takes away his money, and the
other antics depart*

SLIPPER
Nay but my friends, one hornpipe further, a refluence back,
and two doubles forward: what, not one cross-point against
Sundays? What ho sirrah, you yon, you with the nose like   105
an eagle, and you be a right Greek, one turn more, thieves!
thieves! I am robbed, thieves! Is this the knavery of
fiddlers? Well, I will then bind the whole credit of their
occupation on a bagpiper, and he for my money, but I will
after, and teach them to caper in a halter, that have cozened 110
me of my money.   *Exit*

94 *Cicely* stock name for a servant girl or country wench
   Whighton qy. Whittington?
96 *horn* cuckold
99 s.d. *antics* grotesquely costumed dancers
102 *oui, oui* (Q wee wee)
103 *refluence* flowing back (dance movement); *OED's* earliest
   example of the word in this sense
104 *two doubles* steps in dancing
   one cross-point a step in dancing (*OED's* earliest example)
   against as a counter-balance to
105 *yon* (Q gone)
109 *he for my money* he is my choice

94 If my conjecture is correct, *the Whittington* would probably be Ye Olde
Dick Whittington, a fifteenth-century tavern in the Cloth Fair. 'Seeing
that his theatrical career commenced with the booths of Bartholomew
Fair, Ben Jonson must have paid frequent visits to Ye Olde Dick
Whittington' (Leopold Wagner, *London Inns and Taverns*, 1924,
pp. 91–92).

[Act IV, Scene iv]

Enter NANO, DOROTHEA *in man's apparel*

DOROTHEA

Ah Nano, I am weary of these weeds,
Weary to wield this weapon that I bear:
Weary of love, from whom my woe proceeds,
Weary of toil, since I have lost my dear,
O weary life, where wanteth no distress,   5
But every thought is paid with heaviness.

NANO

Too much of weary madam, if you please,
Sit down, let weary die, and take your ease.

DOROTHEA

How look I Nano, like a man or no?

NANO

If not a man, yet like a manly shrew.   10

DOROTHEA

If any come and meet us on the way,
What should we do if they enforce us stay?

NANO

Set cap a-huff, and challenge him the field,
Suppose the worst, the weak may fight to yield.

DOROTHEA

The battle Nano in this troubled mind,   15
Is far more fierce than ever we may find.
The body's wounds by medicines may be eased,
But griefs of minds, by salves are not appeased.

NANO

Say madam, will you hear your Nano sing?

DOROTHEA

Of woe good boy, but of no other thing.   20

NANO

What if I sing of fancy, will it please?

DOROTHEA

To such as hope success, such notes breed ease.

5 *wanteth* ed. (Q wanted)
10 *shrew* person
21 *fancy* love

---

13 *a-huff.* Blusteringly, at a swaggering angle. *OED* cites as a unique
example and glosses 'in a huff', but cf. *huff-cap*, 'blustering' (earliest
example 1597).

NANO
    What if I sing like Damon to my sheep?
DOROTHEA
    Like Phyllis I will sit me down to weep.
NANO
    Nay since my songs afford such pleasure small,   25
    I'll sit me down, and sing you none at all.
DOROTHEA
    Oh be not angry Nano.
NANO   Nay you loathe
    To think on that, which doth content us both.
DOROTHEA
    And how?
NANO   You scorn disport when you are weary,
    And loathe my mirth, who live to make you merry.   30
DOROTHEA
    Danger and fear withdraw me from delight.
NANO
    'Tis virtue to contemn false Fortune's spite.
DOROTHEA
    What should I do to please thee friendly squire?
NANO
    A smile a day, is all I will require:
    And if you pay me well the smiles you owe me,   35
    I'll kill this cursed care, or else beshrew me.
DOROTHEA
    We are descried, oh Nano we are dead.

                Enter JAQUES _his sword drawn_

NANO
    Tut, yet you walk, you are not dead indeed,
    Draw me your sword, if he your way withstand,
    And I will seek for rescue out of hand.   40
DOROTHEA
    Run Nano run, prevent thy prince's death.
NANO
    Fear not, I'll run all danger out of breath.   [_Exit_]

   23 _Damon_ ideal singer of love in pastorals; see Virgil, _Bucolics_, 8
   24 _Phyllis_ ideal young woman of pastorals
   29 _disport_ diversion, merriment
   40 Q assigns to Dorothea
   41 _prince's_ queen's (_OED_ records examples of the word applied to a
      female sovereign from 1560–1650)

JAQUES

Ah you *calletta*, you *strumpetta*, *Maitressa* Doretie *êtes-vous
surprise*? Come, say your paternoster, *car vous êtes morte,
par ma foi*.   45

DOROTHEA

Callet? No strumpet, caitiff as thou art,
But even a princess born, who scorn thy threats.
Shall never Frenchman say, an English maid
Of threats of foreign force will be afraid.

JAQUES

You no *dites votres prièrès*? *Morbleu méchante femme,*   50
guarda your breasta, there me make you die on my morglay.

DOROTHEA

God shield me, hapless princess and a wife,
And save my soul, although I lose my life.

They fight, and she is sore wounded

Ah I am slain, some piteous power repay
This murtherer's cursed deed, that doth me slay.   55

JAQUES

Elle est toute morte, me will run *pour* a wager, for fear me
be *surpris* and *pendu* for my labour. *Bien je m'en allerai au
roi lui dire mes affaires, je serai un chevalier*, for this day's
travail.   *Exit*

Enter NANO, SIR CUTHBERT ANDERSON, *his sword drawn*

43 *calletta* strumpet; Greene has Italianized the English word
   strumpetta ed. (Q strumpet, ta)
   Maitressa should not be emended to Maitresse; cf. *guarda your
   breasta* (IV. iv, 51)
43–44 *êtes-vous surprise*? are you surprised?
44 *surprise* ed. (Q surprius)
44–45 *car . . . foi* because you are dead, on my word
46 *No* ed. (Q me)
50 *dites . . . femme* are not saying your prayers? Zounds miserable
   woman
   Morbleu méchante ed. (Q urbleme merchants)
51 *morglay* sword
55 *slay* (Q stay)
56 *Elle . . . morte* she is absolutely dead
   pour for
57 *surpris* taken
   pendu hanged
57–58 *Bien . . . chevalier* certainly I will go to the king to tell him
   my business, I will be made a knight
58 *lui dire mes* ed. (Q auy cits me)   59 *travail* work

SIR CUTHBERT
  Where is this poor distressed gentleman?   60
NANO
  Here laid on ground, and wounded to the death.
  Ah gentle heart, how are these beauteous looks
  Dimmed by the tyrant cruelties of death:
  Oh weary soul, break thou from forth my breast,
  And join thee with the soul I honoured most.   65
SIR CUTHBERT
  Leave mourning friend, the man is yet alive,
  Come help me to convey him to my house:
  There will I see him carefully recured,
  And send privy search to catch the murtherer.
NANO
  The God of heaven reward thee courteous knight.   70
                    Exeunt. And they bear out DOROTHEA

                                        •

[Act IV, Scene v]

Enter the KING OF SCOTS, JAQUES, ATEUKIN, ANDREW. JAQUES
running with his sword one way, the KING *with his train another*
                                    way

KING OF SCOTS
  Stay Jaques, fear not, sheath thy murthering blade:
  Lo here thy king and friends are come abroad,
  To save thee from the terrors of pursuit:
  What, is she dead?
JAQUES
  Oui Monsieur, elle is *blessée par la tête* over *les épaules*, I   5
  warrant she no trouble you.
ATEUKIN
  Oh then my liege, how happy art thou grown,
  How favoured of the heavens, and blest by love:
  Methinks I see fair Ida in thine arms,
  Craving remission for her late contempt,   10
  Methinks I see her blushing steal a kiss,

  67 *Come* ed. (Q Some)
   5 *Oui . . . épaules* yes sir, she is wounded in the head above the
      shoulders
      la ed. (Q lake)   *over* ed. (Q oues)
      épaules ed. (Q espanles)
  10 *contempt* ed. (Q attempt)
  11 *Methinks* ed. (Q Methink)

Uniting both your souls by such a sweet,
And you my king suck nectar from her lips.
Why then delays your grace to gain the rest
You long desired? Why lose we forward time?　　15
Write, make me spokesman now, vow marriage,
If she deny your favour let me die.

ANDREW

Mighty and magnificent potentate, give credence to mine
honourable good lord, for I heard the midwife swear at his
nativity, that the fairies gave him the property of the　　20
Thracian stone, for who toucheth it, is exempted from
grief, and he that heareth my master's counsel, is already
possessed of happiness: nay, which is more miraculous, as
the noble man in his infancy lay in his cradle, a swarm of
bees laid honey on his lips, in token of his eloquence. For　　25
melle dulcior fluit oratio.

ATEUKIN

Your grace must bear with imperfections:
This is exceeding love that makes him speak.

KING OF SCOTS

Ateukin I am ravished in conceit,
And yet depressed again with earnest thoughts,　　30
Methinks this murther soundeth in mine ear
A threatening noise of dire and sharp revenge.
I am incensed with grief, yet fain would joy,
What may I do to end me of these doubts?

ATEUKIN

Why prince, it is no murther in a king　　35
To end another's life to save his own,
For you are not as common people be,
Who die and perish with a few men's tears,
But if you fail, the state doth whole default,
The realm is rent in twain in such a loss.　　40
And Aristotle holdeth this for true,

26 *melle . . . oratio* his speech flows sweeter than honey

---

21 *the Thracian stone.* Cf. Lyly's *Euphues*, ed. R. W. Bond, II, 90: 'There
is a stone in the floud of Thracia, y^t whosoeuer findeth it, is neuer after
grieued.'
23-25 *as . . . eloquence.* A story told of Pindar, the lyric poet, by Pausanias,
Description of Greece, ix, 23, and by Aelian, *Varia Historia*, xii, 45; and
of Plato by Cicero, *De Divinatione*, I. xxxvi, 76-78.
41-42 *Aristotle . . . least.* Cf. *Nicomachean Ethics*, II. ix, 4, and *Tilley*
E 207 (who does not cite the source).

Of evils needs we must choose the least:
Then better were it, that a woman died,
Than all the help of Scotland should be blent
'Tis policy my liege, in every state,   45
To cut off members that disturb the head,
And by corruption generation grows,
And contraries maintain the world and state.
KING OF SCOTS
Enough, I am confirmed, Ateukin come,
Rid me of love, and rid me of my grief,   50
Drive thou the tyrant from this tainted breast,
Then may I triumph in the height of joy.
Go to mine Ida, tell her that I vow
To raise her head and make her honours great.
Go to mine Ida, tell her that her hairs   55
Shall be embellished with orient pearls,
And crowns of sapphires compassing her brows
Shall war with those sweet beauties of her eyes.
Go to mine Ida, tell her that my soul
Shall keep her semblance closed in my breast,   60
And I in touching of her milk-white mould,
Will think me deified in such a grace:
I like no stay, go write and I will sign.
Reward me Jaques, give him store of crown
And sirrah Andrew, scout thou here in court,   65
And bring me tidings if thou canst perceive
The least intent of muttering in my train,
For either those that wrong thy lord or thee,
Shall suffer death.   *Exit the* KING
ATEUKIN   How much O mighty king,
Is thy Ateukin bound to honour thee: 70
Bow thee Andrew, bend thine sturdy knees,
Seest thou not here thine only God on earth?
JAQUES
  Mais où est mon argent signior?
ATEUKIN
  Come follow me, his grace I see is mad,

44 *blent* disturbed	58 *war* ed. (Q weare)	
61 *mould* body	64 *store* an abundance of	
73 *Mais . . . . signior?* But where is my money sir?		
74 *grace* ed. (Q graue)	*mad* ed. (Q made)	

64 *crown*. All eds. emend to crowns, but I take the word here to be collective. A crown was a coin worth five shillings.

That thus on sudden he hath left us here. 75
Come Jaques,
We will have our packet soon despatched,
And you shall be my mate upon the way.

JAQUES

Comme vous plaira monsieur. *Exeunt* [ATEUKIN *and* JAQUES]

ANDREW

Was never such a world I think before, 80
When sinners seem to dance within a net,
The flatterer and the murtherer they grow big,
By hook or crook promotion now is sought,
In such a world where men are so misled,
What should I do? But as the proverb saith, 85
Run with the hare, and hunt with the hound.
To have two means, beseems a witty man:
Now here in court I may aspire and climb,
By subtlety before my master's death.
And if that fail, well fare another drift: 90
I will in secret certain letters send
Unto the English king, and let him know
The order of his daughter's overthrow,
That if my master crack his credit here,
As I am sure long flattery cannot hold, 95
I may have means within the English court
To 'scape the scourge that waits on bad advice. *Exit*

Chorus

Enter BOHAN *and* OBERON

OBERON

Believe me bonny Scot, these strange events
Are passing pleasing, may they end as well.

BOHAN

Else say that Bohan hath a barren skull,
If better motions yet than any past
Do not more glee to make the fairy greet, 5

76–77 One line in Q
79 *plaira* ed. (Q plera)   *Comme . . . monsieur* As you please sir
81 *dance . . . net* act openly without attracting attention
84 *misled* ed. (Q missed)   86 *Run . . . hound Tilley* H 158
89 *before* ed. (Q for)
  5 *glee* entertainment
    to make . . . greet to salute (?) qy. *gree*; cf. 'to make gree' (to give
    satisfaction)

But my small son made pretty handsome shift,
To save the queen his mistress by his speed.

OBERON
Yea and yon laddie for his sport he made,
Shall see when least he hopes, I'll stand his friend,
Or else he capers in a halter's end.   10

BOHAN
What, hang my son? I trow not Oberon:
I'll rather die, than see him woebegone.

Enter a round, or some dance at pleasure

OBERON
Bohan be pleased, for do they what they will,
Here is my hand, I'll save thy son from ill.   *Exeunt*

[Act V, Scene i]

Actus Quintus . . . Scena Prima

Enter the queen in a nightgown, LADY ANDERSON, *and* NANO

LADY ANDERSON
My gentle friend, beware in taking air
Your walks grow not offensive to your wounds.

DOROTHEA
Madam I thank you of your courteous care,
My wounds are well-nigh closed, though sore they are.

LADY ANDERSON
Methinks these closed wounds should breed more grief,   5
Since open wounds have cure, and find relief.

DOROTHEA
Madam, if undiscovered wounds you mean,
They are not cured, because they are not seen.

LADY ANDERSON
I mean the wounds which do the heart subdue.

NANO
Oh that is love, madam speak I not true?   10

SIR CUTHBERT ANDERSON [*enters and*] *overhears*

LADY ANDERSON
Say it were true, what salve for such a sore?

8 *yon* ed. (Q you); Oberon alludes to Slipper (see V. vi, 40 ff.)
12 s.d. *a round* a dance in which the performers circle; cf. I. Chorus, s.d.
10 s.d. SIR CUTHBERT ANDERSON (Q Ladie Anderson)

NANO
  Be wise, and shut such neighbours out of door.
LADY ANDERSON
  How if I cannot drive him from my breast?
NANO
  Then chain him well, and let him do his best.
SIR CUTHBERT
  In ripping up their wounds, I see their wit,   15
  But if these wounds be cured I sorrow it.
DOROTHEA
  Why are you so intentive to behold
  My pale and woeful looks, by care controlled?
LADY ANDERSON
  Because in them a ready way is found,
  To cure my care, and heal my hidden wound.   20
NANO
  Good master shut your eyes, keep that conceit,
  Surgeons give coin, to get a good receipt.
DOROTHEA
  Peace wanton son, this lady did amend
  My wounds: mine eyes her hidden grief shall end.
NANO
  Look not too much, it is a weighty case   25
  Whereas a man puts on a maiden's face,
  For many times if ladies wear them not,
  A nine months' wound with little work is got.
SIR CUTHBERT
  [*Coming forward*] I'll break off their dispute, lest love
      proceed,
  From covert smiles, to perfect love indeed.   30
NANO
  The cat's abroad, stir not, the mice be still.
LADY ANDERSON
  Tut, we can fly such cats whenso we will.

15 *ripping up* disclosing
17 *intentive* heedful, attentive
25 Q assigns to Dorothea

20–22 *hidden wound . . . coin . . . receipt.* I suspect a bawdy quibble. Note
    Dorothea's reply 'Peace wanton son,' and Nano's reference to 'A nine
    months' wound' (line 28).
27 *wear.* All eds. but Manly emend to *'ware.* But the reference is to the
    consequences of not wearing a maiden's face, i.e. of not being chaste.
31 *The . . . still.* Cf. 'When the cat's away the mice will play' (*Tilley* C 175).

SIR CUTHBERT
How fares my guest, take cheer, naught shall default,
That either doth concern your health or joy,
Use me, my house, and what is mine is yours.   35

DOROTHEA
Thanks gentle knight, and if all hopes be true,
I hope ere long to do as much for you.

SIR CUTHBERT
Your virtue doth acquit me of that doubt:
But courteous sir, since troubles calls me hence,
I must to Edinburgh unto the king,   40
There to take charge, and wait him in his wars:
Meanwhile good madam take this squire in charge,
And use him so as if it were myself.

LADY ANDERSON
Sir Cuthbert doubt not of my diligence:
Meanwhile, till your return God send you health.   45

DOROTHEA
God bless his grace, and if his cause be just,
Prosper his wars: if not, he'll mend I trust:
Good sir what moves the king to fall to arms?

SIR CUTHBERT
The king of England forageth his land,
And hath besieged Dunbar with mighty force: 50
What other news are common in the court,
Read you these letters madam, tell the squire
The whole affairs of state, for I must hence.   *Exit*

DOROTHEA
God prosper you, and bring you back from thence:
Madam what news?

LADY ANDERSON   They say the queen is slain.   55

DOROTHEA
Tut, such reports more false than truth contain.

LADY ANDERSON
But these reports have made his nobles leave him.

DOROTHEA
Ah careless men, and would they so deceive him?

LADY ANDERSON
The land is spoiled, the commons fear the cross,
All cry against the king, their cause of loss: 60
The English king subdues and conquers all.

41 *take charge* take up a military commission
     wait accompany, attend, escort   50 *Dunbar* ed. (Q Dambac)
59 *the cross* the cross of St. George, the English flag

DOROTHEA
  Alas, this war grows great, on causes small.
LADY ANDERSON
  Our court is desolate, our prince alone,
  Still dreading death.
DOROTHEA   Woe's me, for him I moan,
  Help, now help, a sudden qualm   65
  Assails my heart.
NANO   Good madam stand his friend,
  Give us some liquor to refresh his heart.
LADY ANDERSON
  Daw thou him up, and I will fetch thee forth
  Potions of comfort to repress his pain.   *Exit*
NANO
  Fie princess, faint on every fond report?   70
  How well-nigh had you opened your estate:
  Cover these sorrows with the veil of joy,
  And hope the best, for why this war will cause
  A great repentance in your husband's mind.
DOROTHEA
  Ah Nano, trees live not without their sap,   75
  And Clytia cannot blush but on the sun,
  The thirsty earth is broke with many a gap,
  And lands are lean, where rivers do not run,
  Where soul is reft from that it loveth best,
  How can it thrive or boast of quiet rest?   80
  Thou knowest the prince's loss must be my death,
  His grief, my grief: his mischief must be mine:
  Oh if thou love me Nano, hie to court,
  Tell Ross, tell Bartram that I am alive,
  Conceal thou yet the place of my abode,   85
  Will them even as they love their queen,
  As they are chary of my soul and joy,
  To guard the king, to serve him as my lord:

66 *his* ed. (Q her)   67 *his* ed. (Q her)
68 *Daw* revive, bring round
69 *his* ed. (Q h r)
76 *Clytia* ed. (Q Clitia) the Greek form of the name

76 *Clytia* (Q Clitia). In Greek myth an ocean nymph, beloved by the Sun-
  god, who deserted her. She was changed into the heliotrope, a flower
  which is supposed always to turn its head in the direction of the sun,
  and is thus regarded as a symbol of unwavering love (Ovid, *Met.*,
  IV. 234–270).

Haste thee good Nano, for my husband's care
Consumeth me and wounds me to the heart.   90

NANO
Madam I go, yet loth to leave you here.   *Exit*

DOROTHEA
Go thou with speed, even as thou hold'st me dear,
Return in haste.
              Enter LADY ANDERSON

LADY ANDERSON
Now sir, what cheer? Come taste this broth I bring.

DOROTHEA
My grief is past, I feel no further sting.   95

LADY ANDERSON
Where is your dwarf? Why hath he left you sir?

DOROTHEA
For some affairs, he is not travelled far.

LADY ANDERSON
If so you please, come in and take your rest.

DOROTHEA
Fear keeps awake a discontented breast.   *Exeunt*

[Act V, Scene ii]

*After a solemn service, enter from the widow's house a service,
musical songs of marriages, or a masque, or what pretty triumph
              you list, to them,* ATEUKIN *and* JAQUES

ATEUKIN
What means this triumph friend? Why are these feasts?

SERVANT
Fair Ida sir, was married yesterday,
Unto Sir Eustace, and for that intent,
We feast and sport it thus to honour them:
And if you please, come in and take your part,   5
My lady is no niggard of her cheer.   *Exit*

JAQUES
Monseigneur, why be you so sadda, *faites bonne chère,
foutre de ce monde.*

s.d. *solemn service* marriage ceremony
s.d. *triumph* spectacle, pageant   s.d. JAQUES ed. (Q Gnato)
    7–8 *Monseigneur ... monde* Sir ... be cheerful, to hell with the world

---

s.d. *a service.* 'A musical setting of those portions of the church-offices
    which are sung' (*OED*; earliest example dated 1691); cf. *musical songs
    of marriages.*

ATEUKIN

What? Was I born to be the scorn of kin?
To gather feathers like to a hopper crow,   10
And lose them in the height of all my pomp?
Accursed man, now is my credit lost:
Where is my vows I made unto the king?
What shall become of me, if he shall hear
That I have caused him kill a virtuous queen   15
And hope in vain for that which now is lost?
Where shall I hide my head? I know the heavens
Are just, and will revenge: I know my sins
Exceed compare: should I proceed in this?
This Eustace must amain be made away: 20
Oh were I dead, how happy should I be!

JAQUES

Est-ce donc à tel point votre état, faith, then adieu Scotland,
adieu Signior Ateukin, me will homa to France, and no be
hanged in a strange country.   *Exit*

ATEUKIN

Thou dost me good to leave me thus alone,   25
That galling grief and I may yoke in one:
Oh what are subtle means to climb on high,
When every fall swarms with exceeding shame?
I promised Ida's love unto the prince,
But she is lost, and I am false forsworn: 30
I practised Dorothea's hapless death,
And by this practice have commenced a war.
Oh cursed race of men that traffic guile,
And in the end, themselves and kings beguile:
Ashamed to look upon my prince again: 35
Ashamed of my suggestions and advice:
Ashamed of life: ashamed that I have erred:
I'll hide myself, expecting for my shame.
Thus God doth work with those, that purchase fame
By flattery, and make their prince their gain.   *Exit*   40

---

10 *hopper crow* '? a crow that follows a seed-hopper during sowing'
    (*OED*)
13 *is* see *Abbott*, par. 335
20 *amain* ed. (Q a man) immediately
22 *Est . . . état* has your situation reached such a stage
38 *expecting for* awaiting

[Act V, Scene iii]

Enter the KING OF ENGLAND, LORD PERCY, SAMLES, *and others*

KING OF ENGLAND
   Thus far ye English peers have we displayed
   Our waving ensigns with a happy war,
   Thus nearly hath our furious rage revenged
   My daughter's death upon the traitorous Scot,
   And now before Dunbar our camp is pitched,   5
   Which if it yield not to our compromise,
   The place shall furrow where the palace stood,
   And fury shall enjoy so high a power,
   That mercy shall be banished from our swords.

      [Enter DOUGLAS *and others above]*
DOUGLAS
   What seeks the English king?   10
KING OF ENGLAND
   Scot open those gates, and let me enter in,
   Submit thyself and thine unto my grace,
   Or I will put each mother's son to death,
   And lay this city level with the ground.
DOUGLAS
   For what offence? For what default of ours?   15
   Art thou incensed so sore against our state?
   Can generous hearts in nature be so stern
   To prey on those that never did offend?
   What though the lion, king of brutish race,
   Through outrage sin, shall lambs be therefore slain?   20
   Or is it lawful that the humble die,

s.d. KING OF ENGLAND Q gives the king's s.p. as *Arius* throughout
    this scene
s.d. SAMLES a ghost character
  1 *ye* ed. (Q the)
  3 *nearly* closely, severely
  6 *compromise* terms
  8 *enjoy* ed. (Q enuy)

---

  1 s.d. *Arius* at II. ii, 108 appears as the name of the King of Scots. Fleay
(*Biog. Chron. Dram.* I, p. 265), arguing mainly from this confusion of
names, contends that the play was not the work of a single hand, but
that Lodge helped Greene, particularly in V. iv. This seems to me
unlikely, the confusion being explicable by Greene's habitual careless-
ness.

Because the mighty do gainsay the right?
O English king, thou bearest in thy breast
The king of beasts, that harms not yielding ones,
The roseal cross is spread within thy field,   25
A sign of peace, not of revenging war:
Be gracious then unto this little town,
And though we have withstood thee for a while,
To show allegiance to our liefest liege,
Yet since we know no hope of any help,   30
Take us to mercy, for we yield ourselves.

KING OF ENGLAND
What, shall I enter then and be your lord?

DOUGLAS
We will submit us to the English king.

They descend down, open the gates, and humble them

KING OF ENGLAND
Now life and death dependeth on my sword:
This hand now reared, my Douglas if I list,   35
Could part thy head and shoulders both in twain:
But since I see thee wise and old in years,
True to thy king, and faithful in his wars,
Live thou and thine, Dunbar is too too small
To give an entrance to the English king,   40
I eagle-like disdain these little fowls,
And look on none but those that dare resist,
Enter your town as those that live by me,
For others that resist, kill, forage, spoil,
Mine English soldiers, as you love your king,   45
Revenge his daughter's death, and do me right.   *Exeunt*

---

25 *roseal* rose-red
   field the surface of a shield in a coat of arms, on which the
   'charge' is displayed

---

23 *breast* ed. (Q brest). All eds. emend to *crest*, which is heraldically inaccurate. In a coat of arms the crest is that part above the shield and
   helmet. The royal arms contains the lions not in the crest but on the
   shield. As the following line makes clear, Douglas is referring to the
   king's coat-armour, and is therefore correct in his phrase *in* (i.e. on)
   thy breast.

[Act V, Scene iv]

Enter the LAWYER, *the* MERCHANT, *and the* DIVINE

LAWYER

My friends, what think you of this present state,
Were ever seen such changes in a time?
The manners and the fashions of this age,
Are like the ermine skin so full of spots,
As sooner may the Moor be washed white,   5
Than these corruptions banished from this realm.

MERCHANT

What sees Mas Lawyer in this state amiss?

LAWYER

A wresting power that makes a nose of wax
Of grounded law, a damned and subtle drift
In all estates to climb by others' loss,   10
An eager thirst of wealth, forgetting truth.
Might I ascend unto the highest states,
And by descent discover every crime,
My friends, I should lament, and you would grieve
To see the hapless ruins of this realm.   15

DIVINE

O lawyer, thou hast curious eyes to pry
Into the secret maims of their estate,
But if thy veil of error were unmasked,
Thyself should see your sect do maim her most:
Are you not those that should maintain the peace,   20
Yet only are the patrons of our strife?
If your profession have his ground and spring,
First from the laws of God, then country's right,
Not any ways inverting nature's power,
Why thrive you by contentions? Why devise you   25
Clauses, and subtle reasons to except:

5 *sooner* ed. (Q soone)   7 *Mas* vulgar shortening of *master*
8 *a nose of wax* something easily moulded; cf. *Tilley* H 531, L 104,
    N 226   11 *thirst* ed. (Q thrift)   17 *secret* ed. (Q secrets)

4 *ermine . . . spots.* Cf. *Tilley* L 206.
5 *As . . . white.* Cf. *Tilley* E 186.
26 *subtle reasons.* For the derogatory use of the adjective in reference to
    lawyers, see Barnabe Riche, *My Ladies Looking Glass* (1616), sig. I1ʳ:
    '[Lawyers] haue such a number of subtill subtillties, that they do yet
    make more subtill by their subtill handling, that they be able to set the
    Lawes themselues togither by the eares.'

Our state was first before you grew so great,
A lantern to the world for unity:
Now they that are befriended, and are rich,
Oppress the poor: come Homer without coin,   30
He is not heard: what shall we term this drift?
To say the poor man's cause is good and just,
And yet the rich man gains the best in law:
It is your guise, (the more the world laments)
To coin provisos to beguile your laws,   35
To make a gay pretext of due proceeding,
When you delay your common pleas for years:
Mark what these dealings lately here have wrought:
The crafty men have purchased great men's lands,
They poll, they pinch, their tenants are undone: 40
If these complain, by you they are undone,
You fleece them of their coin, their children beg,
And many want, because you may be rich.
This scar is mighty, master lawyer,
Now war hath gotten head within this land,   45
Mark but the guise, the poor man that is wronged
Is ready to rebel: he spoils, he pills,
We need no foes to forage that we have,
The law (say they) in peace consumed us,
And now in war we will consume the law: 50
Look to this mischief lawyers, conscience knows
You live amiss, amend it, lest you end.

LAWYER

Good Lord, that these divines should see so far
In others' faults, without amending theirs!
Sir, sir, the general defaults in state,   55
(If you would read before you did correct)
Are by a hidden working from above,
By their successive changes still removed.
Were not the law by contraries maintained,
How could the truth from falsehood be discerned?   60
Did we not taste the bitterness of war,

30 *Oppress* ed. (Q Or presse)
37 *common pleas* civil actions
40 *poll* practise extortion
45 *war* ed. (Q man)
53 *these* ed. (Q their)
58 *removed* ed. (Q remainde)

30–31 *come . . . heard.* Cf. *Tilley* H 537.

How could we know the sweet effects of peace?
Did we not feel the nipping winter frosts,
How should we know the sweetness of the spring?
Should all things still remain in one estate,   65
Should not in greatest arts some scars be found,
Were all upright and changed, what world were this?
A chaos, made of quiet, yet no world,
Because the parts thereof did still accord.
This matter craves a variance not a speech,   70
But Sir Divine, to you, look on your maims,
Divisions, sects, your simonies and bribes,
Your cloaking with the great, for fear to fall:
You shall perceive you are the cause of all.
Did each man know there were a storm at hand,   75
Who would not clothe him well, to shun the wet?
Did prince and peer, the lawyer and the least,
Know what were sin, without a partial gloss,
We'd need no long discovery then of crimes,
For each would mend, advised by holy men: 80
Thus I but slightly shadow out your sins,
But if they were depainted out for life,
Alas, we both had wounds enough to heal.

MERCHANT
None of you both I see but are in fault,
Thus simple men as I do swallow flies,   85
This grave divine can tell us what to do,
But we may say: Physician mend thyself,
This lawyer hath a pregnant wit to talk,
But all are words, I see no deeds of worth.

LAWYER
Good merchant lay your fingers on your mouth,   90
Be not a blab, for fear you bite yourself.
What should I term your state, but even the way
To every ruin in this commonweal.
You bring us in the means of all excess,

72 *simonies* ed. (Q summonies)
73 *cloaking* pretending, dissembling
79 *We'd* ed. (Q Wee)
81 *Thus I but* ed. (Q Thus but)
     shadow out outline, depict
87 *Physician . . . thyself* Luke 4:23

---

85 *swallow flies*. Not recorded in *OED*, but cf. 'To swallow a spider' (to go
bankrupt), and 'To swallow a gudgeon' (to be gulled).

You rate it, and retail it as you please,   95
You swear, forswear, and all to compass wealth,
Your money is your god, your hoard your heaven,
You are the groundwork of contention:
First heedless youth by you is overreached,
We are corrupted by your many crowns,   100
The gentlemen, whose titles you have bought,
Lose all their fathers' toil within a day,
Whilst Hob your son, and Sib your nutbrown child,
Are gentlefolks, and gentles are beguiled:
This makes so many noble minds to stray,   105
And take sinister courses in the state.

Enter a SCOUT

SCOUT
My friends begone and if you love your lives,
The King of England marcheth here at hand,
Enter the camp for fear you be surprised.
DIVINE
Thanks gentle scout, God mend that is amiss,
And place true zeal whereas corruption is.   *Exeunt*

[Act V, Scene v]

Enter DOROTHEA, LADY ANDERSON *and* NANO
DOROTHEA
What news in court, Nano let us know it?
NANO
If so you please my lord, I straight will show it:
The English king hath all the borders spoiled,
Hath taken Morton prisoner, and hath slain
Seven thousand Scottish lads, not far from Tweed.   5

95 *retail* ed. (Q retalde)
100 *crowns* coins worth five shillings each
105 *minds* ed. (Q maides)
  5 *lads* ed. (Q Lords)

---

105 *minds*. The Q reading makes sense and Manly retains it; however, this
    typical attack on usury and the abuses connected with it (general
    corruption and social revolution) seems to require a general conclusion
    rather than what may be a specific reference to aristocratic inter-
    marriage with the new mercantile class.
  5 *Tweed* ed. (Q Twearde). The River Tweed, forming part of the border
    between England and Scotland; the Battle of Flodden, 9 September
    1513, in which James IV died, was fought near it.

DOROTHEA
  A woeful murther, and a bloody deed.
NANO
  The king our liege hath sought by many means
  For to appease his enemy by prayers,
  Naught will prevail unless he can restore
  Fair Dorothea long supposed dead: 10
  To this intent he hath proclaimed late,
  That whosoever return the queen to court,
  Shall have a thousand marks for his reward.
LADY ANDERSON
  He loves her then I see, although enforced,
  That would bestow such gifts for to regain her: 15
  Why sit you sad, good sir be not dismayed.
NANO
  I'll lay my life this man would be a maid.
DOROTHEA
  [*Aside to* NANO] Fain would I show myself, and change
    my tire.
LADY ANDERSON
  Whereon divine you sir?
NANO   Upon desire.
  Madam mark but my skill, I'll lay my life,   20
  My master here, will prove a married wife.
DOROTHEA
  [*Aside to* NANO] Wilt thou bewray me Nano?
NANO [*Aside to* DOROTHEA]   Madam no:
  You are a man, and like a man you go.
  But I that am in speculation seen,
  Know you would change your state to be a queen.   25
DOROTHEA
  [*Aside to* NANO] Thou art not dwarf to learn thy mistress'
    mind.
  Fain would I with thyself disclose my kind,
  But yet I blush.
NANO
  [*Aside to* DOROTHEA] What, blush you Madam then,
  To be yourself, who are a fained man?
  Let me alone.

  7 *The king* ed. (Q Thinking)
  13 *marks* Scottish coins worth 13s. 4d. Scots
  18 *tire* dress
  26 *learn* reveal

DOROTHEA

> [*Aside to* NANO] Good Nano stay awhile.   30
> Were I not sad, how kindly could I smile,
> To see how fain I am to leave this weed:
> And yet I faint to show myself indeed.
> But danger hates delay, I will be bold,
> —Fair lady I am not, as you suppose   35
> A man, but even that queen, more hapless I,
> Whom Scottish king appointed hath to die:
> I am the hapless princess, for whose right,
> These kings in bloody wars revenge despite.
> I am that Dorothea whom they seek,   40
> Yours bounden for your kindness and relief:
> And since you are the means that save my life,
> Yourself and I will to the camp repair,
> Whereas your husband shall enjoy reward,
> And bring me to his highness once again.   45

LADY ANDERSON

> Deceitful beauty hast thou scorned me so?

NANO

> Nay muse not madam, for she tells you true.

LADY ANDERSON

> Beauty bred love, and love hath bred my shame.

NANO

> And women's faces work more wrongs than these:
> Take comfort madam to cure your disease.   50
> And yet she loves a man as well as you,
> Only this difference, she cannot fancy too.

LADY ANDERSON

> Blush, grieve, and die, in thine insatiate lust.

35 *as you suppose* ed. (Q suppose)
44 *Whereas* where (cf. II. ii, 2)
47 *madam* ed. (Q maiden)
50 *your* ed. (Q our)
51 *she* ed. (Q he)
52 *fancy* indulge in casual amours (as opposed to 'true' love; see line 51)

30–45 *Good . . . again.* The only way to make sense of the text at this point is to move these lines from their position in Q (after line 59) to their present place. The second *Let me alone* (following line 59 in Q) has been excised.

52 *too.* All eds. but Manly emend to *two.* Q makes better Elizabethan sense than the emendation, distinguishing between true love and fancy, i.e. infatuation.

DOROTHEA

Nay, live and joy that thou hast won a friend,
That loves thee as her life, by good desert.   55

LADY ANDERSON

I joy my lord more than my tongue can tell:
Although not as I desired, I love you well:
But modesty, that never blushed before,
Discovers my false heart. I say no more.
Pardon, most gracious princess, if you please,   60
My rude discourse and homely entertain,
And if my words may savour any worth,
Vouchsafe my counsel in this weighty cause:
Since that our liege hath so unkindly dealt,
Give him no trust, return unto your sire,   65
There may you safely live in spite of him.

DOROTHEA

Ah lady, so would worldly counsel work,
But constancy, obedience, and my love,
In that my husband is my lord and chief,
These call me to compassion of his estate,   70
Dissuade me not, for virtue will not change.

LADY ANDERSON

What wondrous constancy is this I hear?
If English dames their husbands love so dear,
I fear me in the world they have no peer.

NANO

Come princess wend, and let us change your weed,   75
I long to see you now a queen indeed.

[Act V, Scene vi]

Enter the KING OF SCOTS, *the English* HERALD *and* LORDS

KING OF SCOTS

He would have parley lords, herald say he shall,
And get thee gone: go leave me to myself:
                    [*Exit* HERALD, LORDS *retire*]
'Twixt love and fear, continual is the wars:

---

55 *her* ed. (Q his)
    good ed. (Q god)

---

56 *my lord.* Dorothea is still in man's clothes and Lady Anderson here
    addresses her accordingly.
 3 *continual is the wars.* No emendation is necessary; see *Abbott*, par. 335.

The one assures me of my Ida's love,
The other moves me for my murthered queen.   5
Thus find I grief of that whereon I joy,
And doubt, in greatest hope, and death in weal,
Alas what hell may be compared with mine,
Since in extremes my comforts do consist?
War then will cease, when dead ones are revived.   10
Some then will yield, when I am dead for hope.
Who doth disturb me? Andrew?

                ANDREW *enter with* SLIPPER

ANDREW   Aye my liege.
KING OF SCOTS
  What news?
ANDREW   I think my mouth was made at first
  To tell these tragic tales my liefest lord.
KING OF SCOTS
  What, is Ateukin dead, tell me the worst?   15
ANDREW
  No, but your Ida, shall I tell him all?
  Is married late (ah shall I say to whom?)
  My master sad: (for why he shames the court)
  Is fled away! Ah most unhappy flight.
  Only myself, ah who can love you more?   20
  To show my duty (duty past belief)
  Am come unto your grace (oh gracious liege)
  To let you know, oh would it were not thus,
  That love is vain, and maids soon lost and won.
KING OF SCOTS
  How have the partial heavens then dealt with me,   25
  Boding my weal, for to abase my power?
  Alas what thronging thoughts do me oppress?
  Injurious love is partial in my right,
  And flattering tongues by whom I was misled,
  Have laid a snare to spoil my state and me.   30
  Methinks I hear my Dorothea's ghost,
  Howling revenge for my accursed hate,
  The ghosts of those my subjects that are slain
  Pursue me crying out, woe, woe, to lust:
  The foe pursues me at my palace door,   35
  He breaks my rest and spoils me in my camp,

26 *Boding my weal* promising my happiness
33 *ghosts* ed. (Q gifts)

Ah flattering brood of sycophants my foes,
First shall my dire revenge begin on you,
I will reward thee Andrew.

SLIPPER

Nay sir if you be in your deeds of charity, remember me.   40
I rubbed Master Ateukin's horse-heels, when he rid to the
meadows.

KING OF SCOTS

And thou shalt have thy recompense for that.
Lords, bear them to the prison, chain them fast,
Until we take some order for their deaths.   45

ANDREW

If so your grace in such sort give rewards,
Let me have naught, I am content to want.

SLIPPER

Then I pray sir give me all, I am as ready for a reward as an
oyster for a fresh tide, spare not me sir.

KING OF SCOTS

Then hang them both as traitors to the king.   50

SLIPPER

The case is altered sir, I'll none of your gifts, what, I take
a reward at your hands? Master, faith sir no: I am a man of
a better conscience.

KING OF SCOTS

Why dally you? Go draw them hence away.

SLIPPER

Why alas sir, I will go away. I thank you gentle friends. I   55
pray you spare your pains, I will not trouble his honour's
mastership, I'll run away.

Enter OBERON, *and antics, and carry away the clown, he makes
pots, and sports, and scorns*

57 s.d. OBERON ed. (Q Adam)
    s.d. *pots* grimaces
    s.d. *sports* amusing gestures
    s.d. *scorns* derisive gestures

51 *The case is altered.* An old joke; for a similar reaction in a similar situa-
    ation cf. *Apius and Virginia*, lines 1128 ff:
        Is there nothing but hanging to my lot doth fall,
        Then take you my rewarde much good doo it you withall . . .
    The jest is there played out at greater length than in *James IV*.
57 s.d. OBERON. Oberon promised Bohan to save his son on this critical
    occasion (see IV. Chorus, 8–10).

KING OF SCOTS

　　Why stay you? Move me not, let search be made
　　For vile Ateukin, whoso finds him out,
　　Shall have five hundred marks for his reward.　　　　60
　　Away with ye. Lords troop about my tent,
　　Let all our soldiers stand in battle 'ray,
　　For lo the English to their parley come.

*March over bravely first the English host, the sword carried
before the* KING *by* PERCY. *The Scottish on the other side, with
all their pomp bravely*

KING OF SCOTS

　　What seeks the King of England in this land?

KING OF ENGLAND

　　False traitorous Scot, I come for to revenge　　　　65
　　My daughter's death: I come to spoil thy wealth,
　　Since thou hast spoiled me of my marriage joy.
　　I come to heap thy land with carcasses,
　　That this thy thirsty soil choked up with blood,
　　May thunder forth revenge upon thy head.　　　　70
　　I come to quit thy lawless love with death,
　　In brief, no means of peace shall ere be found,
　　Except I have my daughter or thy head.

KING OF SCOTS

　　My head, proud king? Abase thy pranking plumes,
　　So striving fondly, mayest thou catch thy grave.　　75
　　But if true judgement do direct thy course,
　　These lawful reasons should divide the war,
　　Faith, not by my consent thy daughter died.

KING OF ENGLAND

　　Thou liest false Scot, thy agents have confessed it,
　　These are but fond delays, thou canst not think　　80
　　A means to reconcile me for thy friend,
　　I have thy parasite's confession penned:
　　What then canst thou allege in thy excuse?

58 KING OF SCOTS ed. (Q omits)
61 *ye* ed. (Q the)
　　troop ed. (Q troupes)
69 *thirsty* ed. (Q thriftie)
71 *quit* repay
　　lawless ed. (Q louelesse)
74 *pranking* ostentatious
　　plumes ed. (Q plaines)
77 *divide* determine (*OED* I 1 d)　　　　81 *to* ed. (Q for to)

KING OF SCOTS
    I will repay the ransom for her blood.
KING OF ENGLAND
    What, think'st thou caitiff, I will sell my child,   85
    No, if thou be a prince and man-at-arms,
    In single combat come and try thy right,
    Else will I prove thee recreant to thy face.
KING OF SCOTS
    I brook no combat false injurious king,
    But since thou needless art inclined to war,   90
    Do what thou darest, we are in open field.
    Arming my battles I will fight with thee.
KING OF ENGLAND
    Agreed, now trumpets sound a dreadful charge,
    Fight for your princess, brave Englishmen:
KING OF SCOTS
    Now for your lands, your children and your wives,   95
    My Scottish peers, and lastly for your king.

*Alarum sounded, both the battles offer to meet, and as the kings
are joining battle, enter* SIR CUTHBERT *to his* LADY CUTHBERT,
with the queen DOROTHEA *richly attired*

SIR CUTHBERT
    Stay princes, wage not war, a privy grudge
    'Twixt such as you (most high in majesty)
    Afflicts both nocent and the innocent,
    How many swords dear princes see I drawn?   100
    The friend against his friend, a deadly friend:
    A desperate division in those lands,
    Which if they join in one, command the world.
    Oh stay, with reason mitigate your rage,
    And let an old man humbled on his knees,   105
    Entreat a boon good princes, of you both.
KING OF ENGLAND
    I condescend, for why thy reverend years
    Import some news of truth and consequence.

89 *brook* ed. (Q tooke) tolerate
92 *Arming* preparing   *my* ed. (Q thy)   *battles* battalions
95–96 Q mis-assigns these two lines to the King of England
96 s.d. *the battles* the armies
    s.d. *to his* beside his (*OED to* A I 5 a)

───

87 *single combat.* Here, a form of trial by combat, a duel to decide a dispute
(*OED*'s earliest example of the phrase is dated 1622).

KING OF SCOTS
    I am content, for Anderson I know
    Thou art my subject and dost mean me good.   110
SIR CUTHBERT
    But by your gracious favours grant me this,
    To swear upon your sword to do me right.
KING OF ENGLAND
    See by my sword, and by a prince's faith,
    In every lawful sort I am thine own.
KING OF SCOTS
    And by my sceptre and the Scottish crown,   115
    I am resolved to grant thee thy request.
SIR CUTHBERT
    I see you trust me princes, who repose
    The weight of such a war upon my will.
    Now mark my suit, a tender lion's whelp
    This other day came straggling in the woods,   120
    Attended by a young and tender hind,
    In courage haughty, yet tired like a lamb.
    The prince of beasts had left this young in keep,
    To foster up as love-mate and compeer,
    Unto the lion's mate, a neighbour friend.   125
    This stately guide seduced by the fox,
    Sent forth an eager wolf bred up in France,
    That gripped the tender whelp, and wounded it.
    By chance as I was hunting in the woods,
    I heard the moan the hind made for the whelp   130
    I took them both, and brought them to my house,
    With chary care I have recured the one,
    And since I know the lions are at strife
    About the loss and damage of the young,
    I bring her home, make claim to her who list.   135

He discovereth her

DOROTHEA
    I am the whelp, bred by this lion up,
    This royal English king my happy sire,
    Poor Nano is the hind that tended me:
    My father, Scottish king, gave me to thee,
    A hapless wife: thou quite misled by youth.   140

109 Q assigns to the King of England   122 *tired* dressed

---

135 s.d. Since her entrance at V. vi, 96, Dorothea must have been kept in
the background, or perhaps is veiled.

Hast sought sinister loves and foreign joys.
The fox Ateukin, cursed parasite,
Incensed your grace to send the wolf abroad,
The French-born Jaques, for to end my days.
He traitorous man, pursued me in the woods,   145
And left me wounded, where this noble knight,
Both rescued me and mine, and saved my life.
Now keep thy promise, Dorothea lives:
Give Anderson his due and just reward:
And since you kings, your wars began by me,   150
Since I am safe, return, surcease your fight.

KING OF SCOTS
Durst I presume to look upon those eyes,
Which I have tired with a world of woes,
Or did I think submission were enough,
Or sighs might make an entrance to my soul,   155
You heavens, you know how willing I would weep:
You heavens can tell, how glad I would submit:
You heavens can say, how firmly I would sigh.

DOROTHEA
Shame me not prince, companion in thy bed,
Youth hath misled: tut, but a little fault,   160
'Tis kingly to amend what is amiss:
Might I with twice as many pains as these
Unite our hearts, then should my wedded lord
See how incessant labours I would take.
My gracious father, govern your affects,   165
Give me that hand, that oft hath blessed this head,
And clasp thine arms, that have embraced this,
About the shoulders of my wedded spouse:
Ah mighty prince, this king and I am one,
Spoil thou his subjects, thou despoilest me: 170
Touch thou his breast, thou dost attaint this heart,
Oh be my father then in loving him.

KING OF ENGLAND
Thou provident king mother of increase,
Thou must prevail, ah nature thou must rule:
Hold daughter, join my hand and his in one,   175

---

165 *affects* feelings   167 *this* her neck
171 *attaint* strike, affect

---

155 *my*. All eds. but Dyce emend to *thy* needlessly, since the King of Scots
    is saying he would give any outward sign to indicate his repentance if he
    thought for a moment he might be forgiven.

I will embrace him for to favour thee,
I call him friend, and take him for my son.

DOROTHEA

Ah royal husband, see what God hath wrought,
Thy foe is now thy friend: good men-at-arms,
Do you the like, these nations if they join,   180
What monarch with his liegemen in this world,
Dare but encounter you in open field?

KING OF SCOTS

All wisdom joined with godly piety.
Thou English king, pardon my former youth,
And pardon courteous queen my great misdeed: 185
And for assurance of mine after life,
I take religious vows before my God,
To honour thee for father, her for wife.

SIR CUTHBERT

But yet my boons good princes are not past,
First, English king I humbly do request,   190
That by your means our princess may unite
Her love unto mine aldertruest love,
Now you will love, maintain and help them both.

KING OF ENGLAND

Good Anderson, I grant thee thy request.

SIR CUTHBERT

But you my prince must yield me mickle more: 195
You know your nobles are your chiefest stays,
And long time have been banished from your court,
Embrace and reconcile them to yourself:
They are your hands, whereby you ought to work.
As for Ateukin, and his lewd compeers,   200
That soothed you in your sins and youthly pomp,
Exile, torment, and punish such as they,
For greater vipers never may be found
Within a state, than such aspiring heads,
That reck not how they climb, so that they climb.   205

KING OF SCOTS

Guid knight I grant thy suit, first I submit
And humble crave a pardon of your grace:
Next courteous queen, I pray thee by thy loves,
Forgive mine errors past, and pardon me.

188 *father* ed. (Q fauour)   189 SIR CUTHBERT ed. (Q L. And.)
192 *aldertruest* truest of all   195 *mickle* much
196 *stays* Q uses a broken ligature ff and thus reads *ffaies*

My lords and princes, if I have misdone,   210
(As I have wronged indeed both you and yours)
Hereafter trust me, you are dear to me:
As for Ateukin, whoso finds the man,
Let him have martial law, and straight be hanged,
As all his vain abettors now are dead.   215
And Anderson, our treasurer shall pay
Three thousand marks, for friendly recompense.

NANO

But princes whilst you friend it thus in one,
Methinks of friendship, Nano shall have none.

DOROTHEA

What would my dwarf, that I will not bestow?   220

NANO

My boon fair queen is this, that you would go,
Although my body is but small and neat,
My stomach after toil requireth meat,
An easy suit, dread princes will you wend?

KING OF SCOTS

Art thou a pygmy born my pretty friend?   225

NANO

Not so great king, but nature when she framed me,
Was scant of earth, and Nano therefore named me:
And when she saw my body was so small,
She gave me wit to make it big withal.

KING OF SCOTS

Till time when,   230

DOROTHEA   Eat then.

KING OF SCOTS

My friend it stands with wit,
To take repast when stomach serveth it.

DOROTHEA

Thy policy my Nano shall prevail:

215 *dead* ed. (Q diuided)   218 NANO ed. (Q L. Andr.)
229–230 One line in Q. Dyce notes: 'Part of the text appears to be
    wanting here'

233–239 On these lines Manly remarks: 'Lines 234, 236 seem to indicate
    that this speech belongs to the King of Scots; and besides, as Kittredge
    points out, one of the kings should speak the closing lines.' Dickinson
    also notes 'by dramatic convention this speech should belong to the
    King of Scots'. But as Rosalind herself demonstrates and points out:
    'it is no more unhandsome than to see the lord the prologue' (*As You
    Like It*, Epilogue).

Come royal father, enter we my tent:
And soldiers, feast it, frolic it like friends,   235
My princes, bid this kind and courteous train
Partake some favours of our late accord.
Thus wars have end, and after dreadful hate,
Men learn at last to know their good estate.   *Exeunt*

[Chorus]

[*Enter* BOHAN *and* OBERON]

BOHAN

And here we'll make ends: the mirk and sable night
Doth leave the peering morn to pry abroad,
Thou nill me stay, hail then thou pride of kings,
I ken the world, and wot well worldly things,
Mark thou my jig, in mirkest terms that tells   5

235 *frolic it* be merry
  1 *And* ed. (Q An)   *here* ed. (Q he)   *make* ed. (Q meete)
    make ends conclude, finish   *mirk* dark
  3 *Thou nill me stay* you are unwilling to stay with me (see *Abbott*,
    par. 220)
  5 *jig* play; cf. II. Chorus, 17; lines 9 and 12 below; and first dumb-
    show, 1, 16; third dumb-show, 8

1–14 Q and all other eds. place these fourteen lines immediately after the
three dumb-shows, between the first two Acts. Manly puts 4. before
line one, and 5. before line nine, explaining as follows:

> Kittredge points out that [third dumb-show, 8] indicates the end
> of the passage relating to the third dumb-show (cf. [first dumb-
> show, 16; second dumb-show, 12]) and is inconsistent with [V.
> Chorus, 9 and 12], and that the presence of *Boh.* before [the first
> half of] V. Chorus, 1, is another proof that a new section begins
> here. We have therefore, not three, but four substitutes for the
> speeches of the Chorus, which now appear at the ends of the Acts.
> But [V. Chorus, 5] implies that there is more of the play, Bohan's
> 'gyg', to come, whereas the whole passage here set apart as 5. seems
> to belong after the fifth Act; and it will be observed that this
> extension of Kittredge's suggestion not only provides a Chorus for
> each Act, but also clears up many obscurities of the text. The
> brevity of these speeches can be no argument against this theory; see
> the end of Act III.

I think Kittredge right and Manly partly wrong; V. Chorus, 5 does not
imply that there is more of the play, but is an injunction to note its
moral. Moreover, lines 1–2 and 11 show these 14 lines to be a unit.
Their position in this ed. provides the play with a logical conclusion
which matches the opening.

The loath of sins, and where corruption dwells.
Hail me ne mere with shows of guidly sights,
My grave is mine, that rids me from despites.
Accept my jig guid king, and let me rest,
The grave with guid men, is a gay built nest.   10

OBERON

The rising sun doth call me hence away,
Thanks for thy jig, I may no longer stay:
But if my train did wake thee from thy nest,
So shall they sing, thy lullaby to rest.

[BOHAN *retires into the tomb. Exit* OBERON. *Song*]

[The Three Dumb-shows]

After the first act

[*Enter* BOHAN *and* OBERON]

OBERON

Here see I good fond actions in thy jig,
And means to paint the world's inconstant ways,
But turn thine ene, see what I can command.

Enter two battles strongly fighting, the one SEMIRAMIS, *the other,* STABROBATES, *she flies, and her crown is taken, and she hurt*

BOHAN

What gars this din of mirk and baleful harm,
Where everywean is all betaint with blood?   5

OBERON

This shows thee Bohan what is worldly pomp.
Semiramis, the proud Assyrian queen,
When Ninus died, did levy in her wars,

7 *Hail* greet		13 *nest* ed. (Q rest)	
14 *rest* ed. (Q nest)		1 *jig* see note to V. Chorus, 5	
3 *what* ed. (Q which for)		4 *gars* causes	
5 *everywean* everyone		8 *levy* ed. (Q tene); qy. *tire* (equip)	

11 *The . . . away.* 'It was a common belief that fairies must vanish at cockcrow' (K. M. Briggs, *The Anatomy of Puck*, 1959, p. 127), but see *A Midsummer Night's Dream*, III. ii, 388–393.

13 *nest.* Bohan calls the grave his nest at line 10, and it is the grave from which he is woken at the beginning of the play.

Dumb-shows. Q and all other eds. place the dumb-shows immediately after the first Chorus, between the first two Acts. But the heading *After the first act* may be merely a printer's note that has crept into the text.

Three millions of footmen to the fight,
Five hundred thousand horse, of armed cars, 10
A hundred thousand more, yet in her pride
Was hurt and conquered by Stabrobates.
Then what is pomp?
BOHAN   I see thou art thine ene,
Thou bonny king, if princes fall from high:
My fall is past, until I fall to die. 15
Now mark my talk, and prosecute my jig.

2.

OBERON
How should these crafts withdraw thee from the world?
But look my Bohan, pomp allureth.

Enter CYRUS, *kings humbling themselves: himself crowned by*
olive, but at last dying, laid in a marble tomb with this inscription:

Whoso thou be that passest, for I know one shall pass,
know I am Cyrus of Persia, and I prithee envy me not this
little clod of clay wherewith my body is covered. 5

All exeunt

16 *jig* play; see note to V. Chorus, 5
s.d. *kings* ed. (Q king)   s.d. *olive, but* ed. (Q Oliue Pat)
  3–5 Q prints as verse (. . . passest,/For . . . I/I . . . Persia,/And
    . . . clay/Wherewith . . .)
  4 *I am* ed. (Q I I am)   *envy* ed. (Q leaue)
  4–5 *this little* ed. (Q thus like a)   5 s.d. *vermium* ed. (Q vermeum)

7–12 Collins: 'The reference here is to the expedition of Semiramis
    against Staurobates, which is told in detail by Diodorus Siculus, II,
    ch. xvi–xviii. Diodorus was readily accessible to Greene by Thomas
    Stocker's translation published in 1599.' [*sic*; 1569]. But Stocker's
    version was in fact a translation from Claude de Seisset's *L'histoire des*
    successeurs d'Alexandre le Grand, itself a translation from a Latin version
    by Janus Lascaris of books 18–20 of Diodorus' *Bibliotheca Historica*,
    with a fourth book from Plutarch (Demetrius). It does not contain the
    relevant material. What Greene's source was I do not know.
3–5 Q prints as verse; all other eds. attempt to reprint them as verse and
    at the same time make them rhyme. Consequently considerable emenda-
    tion is necessary. Once recognized as a prose inscription, most of the
    difficulties vanish. See the inscription on the tomb of Cyrus in Plutarch,
    Alex. 69, in North's version:
        O man whatso'er thou art and whencesoever thou comest, for I
        know thou shalt come: I am Cyrus that conquered the Empire of
        Persia: I pray thee envy me not for this little earth that covereth
        my body.

Enter the king in great pomp, who reads it, and issueth, crieth
vermium

BOHAN
  What meaneth this?
OBERON   Cyrus of Persia,
  M.ghty in life, within a marble grave
  Was laid to rot, whom Alexander once
  Beheld entombed, and weeping did confess
  Nothing in life could 'scape from wretchedness: 10
  Why then boast men?
BOHAN   What reck I then of life,
  Who make the grave my home, the earth my wife:
  But mark me more.

3.

BOHAN
  I can no more, my patience will not warp
  To see these flatterers how they scorn and carp.
OBERON
  Turn but thy head.

Enter four kings carrying crowns, ladies presenting odours to
potentate enthroned, who suddenly is slain by his servants, and
         thrust out, and so they eat.   *Exeunt*
BOHAN
  Sike is the werld, but whilk is he I saw?
OBERON
  Sesostris who was conqueror of the world,   5
  Slain at the last, and stamped on by his slaves.
BOHAN
  How blest are peur men then that know their grave.
  Now mark the sequel of my jig.

  9 *entombed* ed. (Q intombde BM HN VA intombe Folger)
12 *home* ed. (Q tomb BM HN VA tumbe Folger)
  1 *warp* submit (earliest example recorded by *OED* in this sense)
  2 *flatterers* ed. (Q flatteries)
  3 s.d. *four* ed. (Q our)   s.d. *carrying* ed. (Q carring)
    s.d. *potentate* ed. (Q Potentates)   4 BOHAN ed. (Q omits)
    Sike such   *whilk* who (variant spelling of *which*)
  7 *peur* poor (Scottish spelling)
  8 *jig* play; see note to V. Chorus, 5

Printed in Great Britain by
The Garden City Press Limited, Letchworth